NEW WORLD, NEW DREAMS

My Money Story on Both Sides of the Atlantic

This is for the Ladies who feel intimidated by Money and would like to make friends with it, so it sticks around.

Sorana

Table of contents

Chapter 1: The Beginning

My story begins in Romania, a small country in South Eastern Europe – a country of rich history, gorgeous landscapes, friendly people and heart-warming traditions. I am the product of all these ingredients, with a large dose of me (genes, personality and guts). I was also born with a rebel streak a mile long – just well-hidden and under my control. It would show up occasionally, when I needed to make major decisions that affected the trajectory of my life (as you are about to learn from the pages of this book).

As an only child and an only grandchild on one side of the family, I grew up surrounded by love and by adults who were always willing to answer my questions. I always felt too mature for my age (no matter what the age has been); I guess that the "10 going on 30" was me – even though I was not familiar with the expression. I don't remember being childish, though I always admitted to being properly spoiled. I never suffered from temper tantrums as a child. There was never a need to create a spectacle (and I always felt it below my dignity); all I really needed to do was stay on track with what was expected of me – have good grades in school – and I would receive the gifts of my choice and also money.

My earliest memories of my "treasures" include crispy bills, as large as possible. I learned early on that I was less inclined to spend a $100 bill than a $5 or $10 bill. I always exchanged small bills for large ones. I also learned that the crispier and newer the bills (with that "fresh off the press" smell), the more I liked looking at them and therefore I would save them.

Having the kind of bills that I liked to hold and look at, I was more inclined to think through my purchases, and less likely to make impulse buys. This is the best place to mention all these memories date from the "pre-plastic" era, a.k.a. the time before credit cards – not just because of my age; the same thing applied to my parents. Back in those days when you wanted to buy something big, with a higher price than your expendable cash, you had to save the money you needed before buying it because there was no bank to extend you credit – other than for houses, cars or big purchases like that.

One of my fondest money memories from childhood is getting cash rewards for my good grades. Every grade of 10 in elementary and middle school (on a 1 to 10 grading system) was rewarded by my Grandma with $10 each at the end of the school year. I used to rack in some dough in June as I graduated each year… all through middle school.

In my native country of Romania, at the time of my childhood and adolescence, allowance was a foreign concept – you simply did not get money just for the right to be your parents' child (didn't get paid for existing). However, getting paid for chores and good deeds (or grades) was totally appropriate and highly promoted as a tactic to make sure you did more than a few chores (at least in our household). I also remember the cash gifts that I received when I was old enough to spend the money. And I always had this idea of holding on to all the new crisp bills; $100 bills if possible. So, I guess I can fess up to being a collector of pretty banknotes.

I feel that I need to emphasize that this was a time when debit cards had not entered our economy, and credit cards were totally unknown. Reading books now about using cash to discipline yourself to spend less, I can relate to the advice, since I can still remember how hard it was to let go of those crisp $100 bills. The "painless plastic" spending invention had not reached Romania in those days.

Talking to friends here I understood that some of the money lessons they learned growing up included: "money doesn't grow on trees", "you have to work hard for money" and "money is the root of all evil". I remember learning from my dad that it was OK to spend money on the things we wanted because he could always earn more. Looking back, I guess this can be seen as a lesson in abundance, and to some extent, it is. However, he also didn't really keep the money he made, since he always believed there was more coming the next day and the day after that – it just seemed to flow. At the same time, my mom was always the saver. Her prevalent money belief was that we needed to keep some money for later because "you never know" (insert your favorite worry here).

I always described myself as a mutt because of being a mix between a blonde (my dad) and a brunette (my mom), as well as the mix in my gene pool from almost all the provinces of Romania. It is therefore perhaps just as accurate to state that the money lessons that have guided me in life are also a mix between my dad's philosophy of money flowing in and out, and my mom's tendencies to store some away for a later need/big purchase.

I remember money has always been a powerful motivator to do some things that might not be cool or even interesting. All through my childhood and even into adulthood, one of the worst things that could descend on me would be boredom.

Therefore, a monetary reward at the end of a tedious task was always well received and greatly appreciated.

I have recently taken a personality test that names the most significant trait of my personality ACTION. Well, that is such an apt name for my focus on the bottom line, on the outcome. I guess I always knew I was interested in the rewards of a task, in the return from an investment (be it time or money) or in the bottom line in a business venture – I just didn't have a name for this personality "quirk".

Something else I always knew about myself is the fact that I am solution-oriented. When confronted with a problem or challenge, I might panic for a moment or have a bowl of self-pity, but I recover quickly by focusing on what can be done to fix the problem or surpass the challenge. This trait has served me well throughout my entire life, from school, where I had to take multiple exams, to adulthood, when I relocated across the ocean to a city, state and country where the only person I initially knew was my husband.

Throughout my life, I had to learn and relearn multiple rules regarding money. The rules of money were different during childhood – while living under the communist regime – as compared to my adolescence – when democracy came about (or the Romanian version of democracy, anyway). Once I graduated from college and entered the workforce, the rules of money changed again. And when I made the decision to immigrate to a different continent (and made Richmond, VA my home), I had new lessons to learn, as everything was changing AGAIN.

Looking back, I feel that I attended 4 different courses, and they each contributed to who I am today and how I think when it comes to anything financial. I feel privileged and blessed to have had all these experiences teach me such valuable lessons. They allow me to understand situations that may not even be apparent to someone without an outsider's perspective. They have taught me the invaluable lesson of not taking anything for granted.

When the big change in Romania's regime happened, I had to adjust my way of thinking. I was in middle school at the time of the Revolution – this is the name we, the Romanian people, gave the event that resulted in the overthrowing of the communist regime. The good part in the communism was the fact that all people were guaranteed a high-school education and a job after graduation – whether they finished a high school or a university (though higher education wasn't particularly encouraged). The bad part was the food rationing, as well as the restrictions on traveling outside of the country.

The change in regime brought new opportunities, even for a middle schooler like me. It created new options for high school education through the creation of specialty classes – I was able to attend a bilingual English class. I learned early to be decisive and take responsibility for my decisions: my parents let me choose the high school I wanted to attend, as well as my preferred specialty. This was important for an immediate consequence: there was an entrance exam I had to pass, while competing against a lot of students wanting the same thing; and also for a future consequence: my future career might be influenced by the high school I attended, as well as the concentration on some subjects versus others. To this day, I am grateful for my parents allowing me to make that decision.

The structure of high school classes was such that, based on what your major was – Humanistic (more literature, languages, history) or Realistic (more math, physics, chemistry) – you were set on the path to a certain university major, and ultimately a future career. For example, due to my English major in high school and the heavy concentration of languages, history, and geography, I would not be suited for a major in Economical Sciences (the precursor of business school). The university entrance exam for Economical Sciences was based on math, and due to the limited number of classes throughout my high school years, it would have been very hard to keep up with the information received by someone in a Realistic profile high school – even with a lot of tutoring, personal studying, and hard work.

This major change in the way things were done in Romania and the new opportunities that opened up for the people influenced the course of my life. I have always believed that I lived at the best time in history due to the many experiences I was able to have. The opening of the borders led to an opening of the mind – at least for me. The opportunity to travel to England and study there while in college helped me to understand there was a different way to do things, and a different mentality.

Going away to college and living on campus brought the first opportunity to learn how to budget and live on my own. In a country where the family unit is much tighter than the traditional American household, this was a big step in leaving the nest. Even though after graduation I returned to my parents' home for a while (which is the norm in Romania), I learned that I enjoyed my independence. Usually, Romanian students don't have jobs while in college – the class schedule, as well as the unwillingness to hire unexperienced staff make it too high a hurdle. However, between the money my parents provided and the scholarship I earned through good grades, I had finances to practice budgeting skills on.

I learned what it meant to trade partying in the college town for train tickets to go see my friends in my hometown. And I learned how to save for expensive items that I would treasure for many years. Full disclosure on the delayed gratification: credit cards were not an option at the time, so saving for a cool jacket or a fancy pocket book was the only way to get such items. Outside of financing a home or a car, not much credit was available at the time, especially to a student with no earned income. Maybe even that was a lesson worth remembering.

Life in the workforce started for me after college. It taught me soon that working for someone else was not something I wanted to do for the long term. Especially when the person was someone who didn't appreciate my work and didn't care to pay me what my work was worth. After two similar experiences within the field that I really wanted to work in – tourism – I learned that even though I had attended college to work as a travel agent and really enjoyed that career, it would not lead to a financial situation that would allow my dreams to come true.

This epiphany led to my decision to start 2 different homebased businesses while still in Romania. I joined a network marketing company that sold financial products designed to provide retirement funds and act as a life insurance policy in the meantime. And I also started my first Avon business while the company was very new in Romania and had no brand recognition by comparison to what I found after my arrival in the US. I learned that I was good at sales and didn't mind talking to strangers and building relationships.

My first lessons in sales came in seminars with the network marketing company. I learned about lists of prospects and about the "numbers' game" in sales. I had the privilege of spending time with people who had achieved high levels of success and made a lot of money from the business I had just started. I learned that it was possible, and it opened my mind to the opportunities.

In my Avon business, I matched all the requirements for the beginners in sales and qualified for a variety of incentives. I learned how to increase my customer base and how to service them efficiently. I built a thriving business in less than 3 months and kept that business growing until the time I left Romania to relocate to the U.S. And this happened in a country where, according to my mom, "women don't care about lipstick, they worry about putting food on the table". I learned that despite the high prices on food and other necessities, women still cared about the way they looked and still wanted to get gifts for their husbands. This business was built solely on makeup, fragrance and skin care. No other items were available in the Avon brochure at the time.

Learning that it is possible to build a business in network marketing and another in direct sales – in my case, at the same time – opened my eyes and mind to the possibilities. I was born and raised in a blue-collar family and was surrounded by people with an employee mentality. I was quickly aware that I would either have to follow in my parents' footsteps and settle for a job, or I forge my own way without much input from them (because they would not know how to guide me). Needless to say, I chose the latter.

The years in college and the 12 weeks in England while on a scholarship from college helped me build my independence and become a lot more self-reliant than I would have, should I have stayed closer to home the entire time. It also built a sense of being stretched between places instead of firmly rooted to one place. This was also going to serve me well when relocating an ocean and a continent away.

I feel blessed for having parents who − knowingly or not − encouraged me to think independently and to fend for myself. I made the best decisions with the information I had, at those crucial times when it came to choosing majors in high school and college, and in deciding to build businesses instead of chasing jobs. Looking back, maybe I could have taken a different course, but I never had any regrets because the experiences I lived and the lessons I learned molded me into who I am today.

Chapter 2: The Opportunity of a Lifetime

My college years in a big city far away from home were very educational from many points of view. First, from a living perspective: I lived on campus sharing a room with as many as 5 roommates at a time, and had to make sure I maintained good relationships despite personality differences. Then, from a financial perspective: I received money from my parents to take care of my expenses and was also awarded a scholarship for keeping my grades at high levels. This meant I needed to learn how to manage my money (that bad word, budgeting, entered my life) in order to get everything I wanted with the finances I had. Then from a cultural perspective: the city I lived in was even more "Europeanized" than my home town, and this gave me an opportunity to see many possibilities and paths my life could take in the post-college years. And last but not least, from a business perspective: this was the beginning of my networking career. I didn't know it then, but I started to align myself with like-minded individuals and also with people who could and would open new opportunities for me. Even though the word networking had not entered my vocabulary at the time, I was building relationships.

The minimum age to get a driver's license in Romania is 18, but since I grew up in a family that didn't own a car I did not have a license or access to a car I could drive throughout college. The only way for me to get home for a long weekend, a break or vacation was by train. Since most students at that time were in the same situation, I never perceived this as a hardship, nor did I feel I was missing out by not being able to drive. Fortunately, the buses and other means of transport within the city were great, and the intercity trains were somewhat reliable.

Living on campus, over 5 hours away by train from my parents, I learned to prioritize and budget so I could have the things that mattered most to me. I also learned a valuable lesson about earning money – even though I never had a job in college. We were awarded scholarships for good grades, and I enjoyed having some fun money. So, I made it a goal every year to maintain my spot in the top 20% of my class, and even got in the top 5% during my last year (which led to an increase in my scholarship for "merit").

I still remember putting aside the coins I could gather from change I received and from my parents getting some for me, just so I would have enough money to call home during my first year in college. This was the time before cell phones (which may not be hard to believe). It was also the time before the calling cards (which came out during my college years) so I had to go downstairs in the lobby of the dorm with a purse full of quarters (well, the Romanian equivalent of that).

Ever since elementary school, I had decided that I needed to stick with studying since hard, physical labor was not appealing as a means of earning a living. Even apart from the monetary incentives for good grades from my Grandma, I always wanted to be the best and to have good grades. I was also determined to succeed in whatever field I chose, and that was crucial in an academic system that relied on competitive examining for admission into high school, and then college.

For the college spot I coveted I had to perform better than 9 other people who wanted to get the same spot, at an exam comprised of English language and literature, and Romanian geography – these were subjects I had studied in high school. One added element to the college experience was the cost of living in the city where I went to school. Though students attended the classes for free, we each had to figure out where we were going to live. People in the city were renting out rooms in their homes and even entire apartments – this being a large university city – but, for my parents' income, that did not come cheap. The rate of renting a room would have been almost half the monthly income my mom brought home – not including food and utilities.

My mission in passing the entrance exam to get into the college of my choice was not only knocking out 9 other people who wanted the same thing but also doing better than at least 20 other people or more (the ones who would then be my classmates) so that I would be offered a spot in a dorm on campus. The cost of living on campus was a fraction of renting a room in town (the equivalent of $20 or so a month in the U.S.). I came in second place in order of our exam grades and maintained it throughout the years of college, therefore, I always lived on campus. The tradeoff was lack of privacy – having at least 4 other girls in the same room, and one year even 5 others.

I had already learned to embrace my competitive nature during my early years in school. College offered just more opportunities to do so. From earning a scholarship to qualifying for a room on campus, I learned that good academic performance had its perks. When the opportunity of a lifetime presented itself, I grabbed it with both hands. My department had a scholarship program in place with a college in England named the Chichester Institute of Higher Education. Part of the project sponsored by the EU was a 12-week study in England, all expenses paid. Based on the standard of living in Romania at the time, my student status and my parents' income would never had allowed me to have this kind of experience on my own dime. So, I "attacked" the exam that would qualify the "lucky" 15, with all the determination I could muster. And I had lots of it. Therefore, I spent the spring and early summer of my junior year in college studying in England, living on campus in Bognor Regis and learning a lot about the English culture, customs and especially tourism.

This program had been designed by one of my professors in partnership with a professor from the Chichester Institute of Higher Education, a university in England, and it was geared toward my major – Tourism. This was the biggest incentive to go; add to that the experience of living in England for 12 weeks with all expenses paid, and that is too great a prize for the competitor in me not to give it 100%.

From a financial standpoint, this was a treasure not to be wasted. We were given an allowance that, converted in Romanian currency at that time, was the equivalent of twice my father's monthly salary. The money lessons I left England with were priceless. This European exchange program didn't just open doors for the university (by outfitting an entire computer lab) but also opened my eyes to new opportunities.

One of the most important lessons I learned while in England was that things could be different and I could have what I wanted, and that it was not necessarily as hard as I had grown up to believe. I learned that the limitations that I had seen around me while growing up were not valid worldwide and I could break the barriers that had been put around me by my place of birth by just changing my location. Just like in real estate, any good realtor knows that location is critical when selling a house, I understood that location was critical to the realization of my dreams.

My time in England helped me find a serenity inside that I didn't know I was longing for. It also helped me understand that even though my home was where I was born and I would always belong there, it was not where I would live for the rest of my life. I knew I would go toward bigger and better things, only to come to full circle later, and influence my home.

On a professional level, I learned a lot about British tourism and found out that a career in the travel industry would be something I would joyfully embrace – and I did when I first started it, until I learned that it doesn't really help pay the bills. The glamor is only for the people using the services, not for those providing them. Working for different owners of travel agencies, I found out rather fast that I was not meant to build other people's net worth at the expense of mine.

Growing up in a country where a lot of people had to worry how to get enough food and other necessities, during the communists – and then how to get enough money for the food they could now find everywhere, after the communists – I learned a valuable lesson while in England on a scholarship that paid not only for my room and board and schooling but also gave me money to spend on things I wanted. The most valuable lesson I learned was that I LIKED having those choices, those options; I really liked knowing I could achieve things beyond what I had thought possible.

The time spent in England gave me an opportunity to achieve one of my first financial goals. I was able to save enough money from the scholarship money we were provided, to buy a computer. This was in the mid-90's where the price of a desktop was over $400 in a country where the average income was about $200-300 a month. I was going to need a computer for my paper required to graduate from college. Looking back, I realize the trip to England also provided the vehicle to improve my finances and set things in place to achieve other goals, besides visiting a foreign country and learning about their tourism, their custom and traditions, and making friendships that endure.

I guess I should say that I always believed I could achieve anything I wanted. That belief came from my growing up in a family that encouraged me to have self-esteem and to believe in myself. The change now was in the possibilities that I now believed in. My universe was expended by my living in England for 3 months that spring.

The English people also taught me to respect everything around me, whether made by nature or by men. I saw them enjoying the park and feeding the squirrels, and sunbathing on pebbled beaches. And I couldn't help but feel sadness at the memories of all the beautiful mountains and natural wonders of my country, and the beautiful sandy beaches that many of my countrymen took for granted. Even though I had always loved animals and respected nature, I believe my awareness of the damage humans inflict stemmed from my time in England.

Before going on the trip, we spent some time at the college with one of the professors we were going to study with while in Bognor Regis. She asked a question that at the time took us all by surprise. She wanted to find out why the Romanians walked in the streets looking sad or upset, with no smile on their faces. We did not understand what she saw and why she thought people were gloomy. While in England we got used to everyone sharing a smile and a friendly greeting every time we passed them in the street. Only upon my return to Romania did I notice the people I passed by never looked into my eyes or shared a smile – maybe sometimes a greeting though that was rare. In the spirit of full disclosure, I must say that the day of my return home it was dark and rainy. Though, it did hit me at the time. It may have contributed to my determination to move to a different country after college. At the time, England was my first choice.

This was the first time I understood how important it was to be focused and have goals. I could not yet figure out how that would work for me, but I felt unequivocally that I would not spend the rest of my life in Romania. My friends and family thought at first that it was just a phase (a teenager thing) but then they had to admit that I might be speaking the truth – since I was so determined. Though at the time I was planning to move to Western Europe, it ultimately worked out that I would move to the United States.

Being away in college gave me an intensive course in personal finances, along with taking care of the basic needs, such as cooking and washing clothes and all the other domestic things that college students are so fond of that they visit the parents in hopes mom would help out.

I was happy to spend the weeks in England immersed in the culture of the country and the habits of the students. Looking back, I believe the knowledge that I would only be there for a predetermined period, ensured that I enjoyed the time and not really miss my home too much. Since I've lived in the U.S., I miss some of the traditions and my mom's cooking a lot more than I remember from my stay in England.

Being away from home for 12 weeks felt a lot different to my 20-year-old self than the time spent in college, and not just because of being in another country versus only 5 hours away in a different city. It was also due to the cultural differences and the fact that I knew I would not be able to go home and visit every 2 weeks. I guess I could say that it prepared me for the move across the ocean that was to come in a few years, though I had no idea at that time.

During the time spent in Bognor Regis, on the English Channel, we were somewhat isolated in a microcosm formed by the college campus. We did not interact in any significant way with the regular Johns and Marys in the street, other than sharing a greeting and a smile while passing each other. Even though we traveled around England quite a bit, we were still like one big happy Romanian family moving around together.

Probably the closest to a taste of the average English student's life came when we went grocery shopping. At those times we usually went in small groups and bought things to last us for about a week or so. Even this was very different from the grocery shopping we did back home, where everything was bought fresh, almost daily. This was my first experience buying sliced bread (the really cheap kind used for toast – which I had never even seen before). And I still remember (almost 20 years later) the surprise of noticing moms filling up their vans with groceries for the week, and putting many loaves of sliced toast bread in the grocery bags. Bread that was over 2 days old was not something we were ever interested in eating back home – and not that it was bad, we just never bought enough to last that long; there was always fresh bread within a 5-minute walk.

My most vivid money memory related to the time that I spent in England is connected to the English students we befriended there. There was a small pub on campus where many of us spent time in the evenings, with one or more pints of beer, or sodas. One could frequently hear an English student complain about lack of money for beer for the week.

Even for someone who might want to buy many pints each night it was not hard to make money, considering the light schedules we all had, and the many opportunities for hourly temp jobs available in town. We were all surprised by the English students being broke once we figured that one day of work with one of the temp agencies in town would pay more than enough for beer for the week. In fact, the pay was sufficient to cover rent in town for the week (at least for the student prices we were told). Coming from a country where students could not work – both due to a lack of time (loaded schedules) and a lack of interest from employers (everyone wanted experienced workers) – the fact that there were jobs they could do and financial comfort to be had, yet the students still complained about lack of funds, is still one of the unresolved mysteries of my youth. Since hindsight is always 20/20, I can now compare their attitude with what I have seen in the U.S. – and it is related to the entitlement mentality. Even though they had options to remedy the problem, they hated the effort it would take to get it done.

Chapter 3: The Start of Adult Life

Graduating from college was similar to a rite of passage for me since I perceived it as a transition toward independence. Even though grown children don't leave the parents' house upon graduating in Romania, traditionally, the end of the school years meant starting the adventure in the workforce. I understood that was not a glamorous prospect, but it still seemed like a great time to figure out what adult life was all about. The one thing I knew about my future among the working adults was that I was not built for the traditional 9 to 5 office work – though I might have to start there.

After the college years when I was unable to work any job – partly because the schedule would not allow me to work any regular hours, and mostly because the majority of employers were not interested in hiring college students – I felt ready to "earn my keep". As an only child, I was never told I needed to contribute financially to my parents' household. This gave me the flexibility to look for the job I wanted instead of settling for a job I just had to accept.

The first 2 jobs I had were in the field I had studied, in the position I was prepared for, through my major in college. I had graduated with the understanding that working as a travel agent in a traditional agency was where I wanted to start my career. So that was where I headed first. I learned the first paradox of job seekers while looking for my entrance in the industry I wanted to be a part of: most of the employers were not interested in hiring someone who lacked experience. It didn't matter to them that I needed to start somewhere in order to get said experience.

After having a few prospective employers tell me that I lacked the experience, I found someone willing to give me a chance. That job lasted a few months in the summer and taught me that I could not work for someone whom I didn't respect, for someone cutting corners and embracing the policy of "we are not doing this because it costs me money" (regardless of the potential gain).

Even though the products offered in this first travel agency were not many, I learned the basics as I dealt with clients, boss, and partner agencies. I also had contact with enough basic accounting to apply the knowledge from college and realize the financial situation of the agency. Started as a spinoff from the retail store the owner had, it was simply a toy for his daughter – a no longer amusing and easily discarded toy. The owner was not interested, nor had the knowledge to build up the business in the agency. And I was too new and inexperienced to be able to grow this agency – despite my passion for travel, as well as the business side of tourism.

That first summer among the working adults, I learned that most employers were not willing to train an inexperienced graduate. Therefore, I figured I just had to start somewhere – by accepting a job with amateurs in the tourism industry. And it got better with the second job since it was easier to get hired – now I was no longer inexperienced. I worked in 2 more travel agencies in Romania, and with every new agency, the people I was working with were more experienced and able to teach me more about the business. Each employer did the business closer and closer to the way things should have been done.

The second travel agency I worked for had found success by specializing in travel groups to Turkey – the owner was from Turkey and had moved to Romania for business. This was my first lesson dealing with a foreign employer – and one who believed to always be right to boot. After a very successful spring and summer, he was ready to rack in a lot more dough through the fall. Unfortunately, a big earthquake in Antalya (a touristic region where most of the vacations were sold for) put an end to the travel in the area, and slowly killed the business I was a part of. The only "souvenir" I have left is a friendship with my former colleague.

I moved on to a bigger agency once the owner closed down that business, and I was now working with people who knew the industry and were willing to train me. My first thought when I saw the operation of this new travel agency was that I had learned how not to do business in the travel industry, and now it was time to learn how to do it. I was there for almost a year. I learned a lot about the travel agency, about the rules and regulations, and about running a satellite office. I learned how to build a business for the travel agency by having a variety of services, and not just one that the agency depended on. I felt that I learned so much about the business side of travel that I became a "terrible" traveler, always noticing everything that was not done right. And it was there that I met the man who was going to change my life and influence my future.

The employer in the last agency where I worked, had a larger company and it was a travel business – no mixing it with a retail store and not started because of a few good friends in one area of a foreign country. He had been in the business for some years, and many of the agents were also experienced. This gave me an opportunity to learn a lot more about the industry from people who knew the business. I learned about group trips, package vacations and also the insurance travelers should have while abroad. Maybe I started in the financial and insurance industry back then, with a slow slide in the personal insurance – and not by joining the life insurance broker later that same year. I learned how to be a consultant, advising travelers about the protection they had to have and the protection that was nice to have. It was also during my time with this last agency that I found out that I liked knowing how the business worked, not just being able to present the products.

A very important money lesson from the time spent at one of the travel agencies, is related to lending money to a friend in need. I made friends with a family who owned a currency exchange office. They had some troubles with their company and asked for my help and my co-worker's. We believed that being a good friend meant being there for them and helping them out by lending them money to get over the obstacle in their business. We shared our savings with the belief we would get the money back within a short period. Unfortunately, we were deceived and lost the money we lent them. This experience wiped out the meager savings I had managed to set aside. I was determined never to loan any money, no matter the closeness of the relationship – unless I was giving the money away, with no expectations of getting it back. I have stood by that resolution and intend to continue doing that. I have donated money to friends since then but never lent with the expectation to get it back. This is a lesson taught by other financial leaders in the U.S. (as I was going to find out later): don't give your friends money you cannot afford to lose;

always lend with the knowledge that you might never get it back from them.

The experiences with the travel agencies also served as lessons of what I did not want to do in my career and my life. Though I enjoyed the work and loved being in the travel industry, I realized that I didn't care for working for employers who were not willing to take care of their employees when it came to salary; and I found out that I much rather preferred starring in my own movie to being an extra in someone else's. This made the decision to start looking for other opportunities and to open my mind to possibilities outside the traditional employment that much more logical. And this is how my introduction to network marketing (at the time known as MLM – multi-level marketing) happened: first in one company (in the financial industry) and then in another (in the beauty space).

While working a job and starting a network marketing business in financial services, as well as a direct sales business with Avon, I discovered that I enjoyed participating in different companies and building my own businesses. Needless to say, the job became my least favorite work. I really enjoyed working in a travel agency, and I started dreaming of owning one someday in the future; I just didn't enjoy building someone else's dream, who didn't show any appreciation for the effort. So, the closing of the satellite office came as a solution to a dilemma I was facing: how to find more time to allocate to my fledgling businesses.

This was the first time I became fascinated with making money in the financial industry and building a business through sales. My biggest hurdle in the financial business was lack of credibility due to my young age. My target market was comprised of my parents' friends while I was still a very young-looking 21-year-old, closer in appearance to their children. I remember wishing to look older – and a few gray hairs would have been welcome. Ha, if only my younger self could see me now! A smile comes on when I think back to the many times I wished I could have the credibility of another colleague – at the time she was not much older than I am currently. I remember her success as an incentive to believe that it was possible but also as a challenge that I was not sure how to surmount. This was the time when I started wearing makeup, and I bought my first suit jacket – all in an effort to look a little older and more business-like than my age would normally project. We have a saying in Romania: "Be careful what you wish for, because you might just get it" – well, now I am older and earned every white hair on my head. Though I must admit: my credibility level has gone up.

Even though this business venture did not prove to be a financial success for me, it was a great mindset success; it opened my eyes and mind to the possibilities. By meeting successful people in this business – a company that was relatively new in Romania, selling a product that Romanians were not educated to plan for, an intangible product at that – I learned that success is dependent on each person, and you can achieve anything you put your mind to... as long as you are willing to commit the effort necessary.

My Avon business was more successful than I even thought possible. Maybe I didn't have very high expectations going in, since I had only heard of the company for a short while, and only learned that it was a cosmetics company just prior to signing up. Plus, the company was very new to Romania (which actually was an advantage for them, since they experienced tremendous growth). At the time in Romania, recruiting was not available to Avon representatives, so my focus was entirely on sales.

I learned that I had no problem talking to strangers and built a big enough client base to achieve all the incentives available to new representatives – twice. Oh, that is correct: I got my mom signed up and handled the sales. She was so surprised to have been so wrong. She had predicted that women didn't care for lipstick, they were too worried about putting food on the table and taking care of their kids and husbands. Well, for someone who never used lipstick… how would she know?! And it was so much fun proving her wrong and turning her into an Avon customer as well.

We learned together that no matter the level of income or the state of the economy, women still want to feel good about themselves, and a great self-image goes a long way toward that direction. Even colleagues my mom had known for years surprised her by becoming clients – proving that you never know everything about someone until you talk to them about that aspect of their life or personality.

Income taxes and self-employment are very different beasts in Romania, therefore I will not go into details on them here. I need to mention that running my Avon business taught me about the importance of cash flow and the difference between wholesale and retail prices, from a seller's perspective. Both lessons still serve me well in my new life across the pond.

Both of these businesses were my "side hustles" at the time, especially in a family with a traditional view on life-work plan: go to school, study hard, get a job and work until you retire from that company (or maybe a second one, at most). Sounds familiar? Well, I learned the explanation of the mentality by reading Robert Kiyosaki's book, "Rich Dad, Poor Dad" many years later, while living in the U.S.

With this in mind, it is easier to understand why, once my job ended with the travel agency, I accepted the offer to work with a Korean family living in my city: tutor the kids for school and teach them English, and teach the parents Romanian. It was a challenge and an experience from many points of view, most notably the cultural differences. I had some experience with tutoring from teaching English to Romanians while in high school but this was a more difficult task. I learned that explaining my native tongue was a lot more complicated. I hope I helped them get some knowledge of language and culture. I sure gained a lot of knowledge about living in a foreign country and getting integrated into that culture. Despite the success of my "side hustles" I was not making the progress toward financial comfort, let alone the financial freedom, that I wanted. I understood that it was harder to reach my financial goals in Romania than it would have been in Western Europe – I had the experience in England confirming that. So, I decided that I was going to work on a plan to go out of the country to work, preferably in England (even though at the time that was probably the hardest European country to immigrate to). Another option was working on a cruise ship, as many of my friends were doing. That had a certain appeal, since I have always loved traveling and seeing new countries.

While I interviewed with a couple of companies and talked to my friends to get as much information as I possibly could on the employment abroad, I spent my nights on the internet – in a country where computers were not in every home (and certainly not in mine – it had been stolen in a break-in). I kept in touch for many months with my now-husband and we started talking about a life together. It seemed unreal that he was half a world away but still we connected on such a profound level. So, my life changed again.

Funny how things work out: I had a plan and was working toward my goals, and then was derailed. I left my life and everyone I knew to come to a new world (for me) and be with a man who was now my husband. I had no idea what a culture shock I would have! I was somewhat prepared by my experience in England – or so I thought. That idea went out the window once I landed.

Chapter 4: The New Beginning

I arrived in the post 9/11 U. S. with $100, 2 bags and a heart full of dreams. I trusted that I would be OK and that I was on my way to greatness. I had never been in the U.S. before the terrorist attacks, so the airport security was just a "normal" inconvenience to me. It was exciting and terrifying at the same time. Having to take my shoes off was the most notable difference from my previous flights (to England, back in college). I also had to talk to custom authorities both in Amsterdam (my layover) and in Detroit upon my first landing in the U.S.

Once I had a chance to grasp the idea that my life had changed yet again, and that I now had total control of my future without the benefit of well-meant "encouragement" toward one choice versus another (from my parents), I had to put my big girl panties on, and decide what my next move would be. I realized that even though I had enjoyed building my businesses, I would need to start by having a job while I learned the lay of the land. The main obstacle starting off in this new world for me was not the fact that I knew nobody besides my husband, but the inability to get around without a car – common transportation was inexistent (still is) in the county where I resided, and I did not drive when I first got to the greater Richmond, VA area.

From the information provided by the Immigration Services, I knew that I would be receiving my Green Card shortly, and that it represented the right to work and reside in the U.S. At the time, I had no idea that citizens and residents of my new country had an identification number for tax purposes called a Social Security number and that I needed to apply for one, let alone have a Social Security card to show prospective employers. Had I known that, I would have made a bee-line for the nearest Social Security office to apply. However, coming from a country with a totally different system, I was clueless. And for a husband who took this system for granted and never had to worry himself with understanding it, explaining to me the importance of a Social Security card, number, or anything, was not even a thought.

Being very much a woman of action, I will probably always look back at those first couple of weeks in my new country as a wasted time when it comes to taking steps toward a new career because I did not know what I did not know and the result was that I did not take the steps I needed as soon as I could have. I only found out about the necessity of the Social Security number once I started talking with potential employers. If this book gets into the hands of newcomers to the U.S., I hope it will serve as a guide to what they need to know. Even though, as a new immigrant, you receive a package with information from the embassy or the USCIS office you deal with, the stuff they share is not designed to inform 100%, and it is not as self-explanatory as one might think. And if you are not familiar with the laws and rules of U.S. living, you may not be aware of some things, and therefore, you would not know what to expect or to look for.

I learned quickly that the things I needed to know in order to take the proper steps to integrate my work life with the life of the average American, were very different from what I expected and, of course, from what I had known for my whole life. Everything was done differently; from the way we figured out how to get to a place my husband did not know where it was, to the way I now had to prospect for jobs, to finding the people who provided the services we needed – such as car repairs (later, I will talk more about my car stories; there are quite a few lessons there).

The first document I received as a permanent U.S. citizen was my Green Card. I found the name interesting because in Romania, while working in tourism, I had become familiar with the term for a very different reason: when traveling abroad by car, Romanians were supposed to purchase a Green card for their vehicle – this was a type of car insurance while out of the country. As a new immigrant, I learned that the American Green Card was essential in proving my legal status in my pursuit of employment. The USCIS – then the INS – was very prompt in sending the card, and I had it within a month from my arrival. This sounded wonderful, since I was excited to join the workforce. As I started talking to potential employers however, there was a question of a Social Security card that was a foreign notion to me. I learned that it was a must for any employee who was a citizen or legal alien resident in the U.S. – and that was the very first time I ever heard of such object.

The mystery of the Social Security number revealed, I found myself in front of the Social Security agent who took my information and promised to process my request for a number as soon as possible. I was also told that it took up to 3-4 weeks to receive the card in the mail, but I would be able to call and find out my number after about 2 weeks, and I could provide that number to potential employers to verify my employability status.

Now I was about to learn a lesson in American bureaucracy – and the fact that I had not left incompetence back home, across the Atlantic. After I waited the "necessary" 2 weeks, I called the Social Security office and started inquiring about my status and my number. I was told a couple of times that it was still in process, and I renewed my inquiries every couple of days. After about a week, I had the luck (even though it seemed the opposite at the time) of getting in touch with an agent who was very brusque and very prompt in telling me that there was no way to find out my SSN before receiving my card in the mail. At my insistence to find out the whereabouts of the said card, she also informed that she was unable to track down my paperwork and I needed to get back to the Social Security office and reapply for a card and a number.

At this point, my American born-and-raised readers could feel my pain and frustration in dealing with the government bureaucracy. At the time, I went to the Social Security office with a heavy heart and a little doubt in my mind that I was on the right path to greatness and accomplishment on the professional level. However, when you don't have a choice, and don't know any different, you follow the instructions of the person who has the authority to tell you what to do, and whom you perceive to be a specialist – based on the power of their function and/or job. As I write this paragraph and think back to that day and the feeling in my heavy heart, I can relate to many prospects and clients I met over the years in the financial and insurance industry. I understand how they would follow the advice of the person they get to talk to because that person's role in the industry recommends them as a specialist and therefore someone whose advice should be followed.

Since I was a person of action and all my previous experience had been in a country where I knew the rules and could play the game with confidence, and having a husband short on patience, the experience of the repeat visit to the Social Security office left me a little short on self-confidence for a while. It was the first time I felt like a stranger in a strange land, and the first time I ever doubted my self-confidence.

Funny how I was not even expecting to write about this experience as I was unfolding this chapter in my mind, and now I have allocated over 2 pages to it. However, I feel it is important to understand that many lessons that have molded me into the professional I am are still etched in my mind and will come to the front with but a little nudge.

I renewed my search for my first American job armed with the knowledge that my paperwork was indeed in process with the Social Security Administration. I was simply stating to the prospective employers that my card was on its way and I would be able to provide it shortly for their records. And this helped raise my confidence level back to normal. I felt again that I had a handle on what was going on, and that I was no longer in the dark about the rules and laws I was expected to follow in my new country.

The first business owners to give me a chance at building my American dream of a steady paycheck were a couple who owned an antique store with a bridal registry. It was a novelty for me since I had no experience with the custom of buying gifts off a list to be delivered to a bride-to-be. Money lesson for my American readers: in Romania, a bride and groom receive mostly money as their wedding gift from the guests at the wedding, on the night of the wedding, not before. The only presents that are not in the form of cash might be a car or an apartment from their parents or godparents – and that is not a normal occurrence (only for rich people).

I found out pretty soon that the American dream is built on working more than one job at a time, if you want to have any money left after paying the regular monthly bills. I found a job in the front desk department of a hotel. It gave me a chance to learn the travel industry from the other side of the equation. It was a good experience – in all three of the hotels I worked. I learned a lot about life as an employee in the U.S: not really different from the life of an employee in Romania. The pay is as small as the employer can get away with – at least in the hotel industry. The hours are cut during the slow season; nobody gets overtime if it can be avoided. The exciting pay raise is nothing to write home about.

It took me about a year to learn the way life unfolds in America. During this time, I learned that everything was different from the way I was used to doing things, and I mean everything. From the way we found out how to get to a place we didn't know (by looking up directions online vs asking the people at the company where we were going), to the fact that when you receive a call on the cell phone, your provider deducts minutes from your plan. My friends back home are still laughing over this one.

From my position as an employee I learned about getting paid through direct deposit – we never had that in Romania while I was working there. I also learned about income taxes and having to file a Form 1040 by April 15 – in Romania, only self-employed people and companies have to file their taxes, everyone else just has them deducted from their paycheck.

The biggest adjustment was probably the fact that I could not walk to any destination, I had to use a car; so, I learned how to drive once I got a little bit used to the way the roads were. Switching from the "go to the left or the right" system to the "go north or go west" system took some adjusting, even for someone who graduated from the Geography Department of the University.

As soon as I arrived in the U.S., my husband asked me if I wanted to continue my education and enroll in any classes. I was (and still am) firmly convinced that I had finished my college education for free in Romania, and never had a desire to go back to classes that I now had to pay for. Since the major I studied in college was my dream subject, there was never any question of going to study a different field.

I had a few jobs as I was getting settled in my new life, as it took me a while to learn the way things are done in the U.S. – including learning how to drive. One of the lessons I learned was the fact that a paycheck from a hotel front desk job does not stretch very far, and therefore I had 2 and even 3 of those jobs at times. There were months when I worked so much that a day off meant working only one job.

Once I learned how to drive, I decided to get a car of my own. My husband never believed in making payments, and would only buy as much car as he could afford to pay for upfront. Even though I totally agree with the school of thought that teaches not to take on consumer debt, buying just the car you can afford to pay in full can be a problem waiting to happen when you can only afford to pay less than $1000 for it. After our experiences with 7 cars dying in my first 2 years in the States, I was determined to deal with a car payment in exchange for the peace of mind of having reliable transportation.

Buying a car brought on another teaching moment: credit history and buying something on credit. Before shopping for a car, I had already started using a credit card through my Avon business – I had been approved for a $500 credit limit. I don't remember who first told me I needed to build my credit, but this was the reason for opening the card. And I was very pleased with the way I was working on my credit history, especially considering that I had been in the U.S. for less than 2 years. Well, my pride in doing the right thing was shot to smithereens when I was told it was very hard to receive a credit to buy a car without someone cosigning for the loan, due to the lack of a 7-year credit history on my part. The confusion must have been written all over my face when I restated that I had only been in the country for 2 years and already had a 6-month history on one card. I was calmly told that it was not enough and that a bad credit history was better than no credit history.

This provided an opportunity for a new lesson in my new adoptive country: I accepted a loan at a high interest rate in order to be able to get a more reliable car than what cash could buy me at that time. I took the loan, made payments for the first 6 months while building some credit history, and then refinanced it through a credit union for a lower rate. This process in itself was another lesson: credit unions are similar to banks but have some more lenient rules on the loans to their members. Since we didn't have credit unions in Romania, it was an opportunity to learn some things about the American banking system.

When I needed to replace that car a year later, I again had to apply for credit, and this time it was a totally different experience. A dealership that had flatly refused my business a year prior was now happy to extend enough credit to me to pay off the first car and buy a new one. And the interest rate was 0% for the entire length of the loan, since they were running a special offer at the time.

I am now aware that most financial gurus advise that we all buy second-hand cars because new cars lose value the minute they are driven off the lot. While I'm not debating the point, I have to say that for me the most important thing was reliability because I always had to have a good car. Also, my first brand new car was my only car for 10 years, and I had it for the majority of that time without a car payment. Plus, I had to spend less than $2000 for repairs – excluding the wear and tear on things like tires and brake pads. I probably would have had to pay more, had I bought used cars that I would have had to replace a few times. My first new car convinced me to replace it with the same make and model, just a newer one – 10 years later. Something I heard a long time ago: keep a winner, don't get rid of it.

Chapter 5: The Decision

As I relocated across the pond and left everything and everyone I knew, I decided that all the sacrifices I made by tearing myself away needed to be worth it. I needed to make sure I built a life and career better than what I could have achieved in Romania in the short run. So, I figured the best thing to do was learn as much as I could about money and building a business. And the first book I came across was "Rich Dad, Poor Dad" by Robert Kiyosaki. I have heard a lot of successful people credit this book for a change in their life, and I can add my voice to theirs. It was an eye-opener for me – a window into the American ideas of business ownership, and how to get a piece of the American dream. By the time I read this book I had already started my Avon business here in the U.S. and had already decided that I wanted to be a business owner.

Based on my experience with direct selling, I considered that the best path into entrepreneurship for me. I didn't know anything about business structures and how to build a business from scratch, so starting with a company that would give me the tools to succeed proved to be the best route. I later learned from famous entrepreneurs that working with network marketing companies to get the business training is a recommended strategy. I made the right decision, though for me it was based more on instinct than on knowledge at the time. With this new adventure, I learned the term self-employed.

After running myself ragged working 3 jobs in the front desk department of 3 different hotels, I found an opportunity to work as a self-employed insurance agent and enrollment agent with a life insurance company. I received a lot of training in sales and built a customer base that I'm still proud to think about, many years later. What attracted me to the company was the opportunity to talk to people who had expressed some interest in the information, and not have to prospect in order to find those people myself. What kept me going with the company for 8 years was the opportunity to help families ensure they were safe and would be taken care of in the event of an unexpected death in the family.

As I started my journey as a self-employed professional, I also had to learn a lot about both taxes and saving for retirement. Though not really taught in the company, we were given the opportunity to save money through buying company stock. I decided to take the offer, and I still have shares with the company to this day. Working there, I knew it was a good company, and in an industry that will not become obsolete – life insurance. A mentor later told me that it was risky to have stock in one company, and that managed money was a better choice. Looking back at the opportunity to invest in company stock, I appreciate the fact that it was an option but not the only choice that was given. The reason I invested was because I knew the company was solid – no blind faith out of me; also following Warren Buffet's example, since he had invested around that time.

While I will always encourage people to seek mentors and follow their advice, I do believe that trusting your instinct comes before blindly following someone else's advice – I believe there is no "one-size-fits-all" when it comes to anything regarding your own life: health, medicine, finances, family, or any other decisions that will influence your life. I believe that no one knows better than you what is best for you. With that said, I do feel very strongly about making informed decisions and looking before you leap. Once you do your research and are satisfied that you have all the pertinent information, you can make the best choice. It is actually a good idea to seek guidance, just don't follow the advice blindly.

During my years with the life insurance company I worked some long hours, sometimes even 6-7 days a week. Yes, the schedule was just as hectic as it had been back in the days of my 2-3 jobs at a time. The most prominent difference was the fact that now I only worked my schedule, and was never responsible for filling in when someone else didn't feel like showing up. I think this was the first thing I liked about my new career. I knew I would go to work, do what I had scheduled for that day, and then get back home. I saw 2 major advantages to this: I didn't have to stick around waiting for a certain time to come (like 5 pm for most professionals), and I didn't have to do someone else's job because they were not getting stuff done.

I started my career working as an agent and then moved into the management track. I also learned something else at the life insurance company that was 180 degrees different from the traditional job: nobody was given a leadership position, they were all earned. I didn't have to worry about having to train my new boss (as I had to do in the past) any more than I had to worry that someone I trained would later become my boss by me being passed over for a promotion. All I needed to do was work hard and lead by example. The company was definitely not built on the principle of "do what I say, not what

I do"! In fact, it was the exact opposite. Even the CEO and the Chairman had started as agents and had built and trained teams all across the country, thus earning their positions instead of someone deciding to give them the titles.

During my years with the life insurance company, I learned that I am very detailed with paperwork and I thrive on making sure all the T's are crossed and all the I's are dotted. Working in a highly regulated industry, I understood that this was a great trait to have. The longer I talked to families about their need for life insurance, the more I became interested in the situation of life insurance coverage in the U.S. because the situations I came across in the field could be divided in a few distinct categories: families who didn't have life insurance, families with only one of the spouses aware of the family finances, and families who had to deal with a funeral (or more) or knew someone close who did it, when they didn't have any life insurance for the loved one who had died.

There were times when I wished I could do more for the families but was not able to help protect them with life insurance because the person who needed the coverage had a medical condition that prevented them from qualifying for life insurance. I found out that a lot of people feel that there is no rush to get life insurance – since, as someone once told me "I want to cancel my life insurance because I'm not using it". Unfortunately, as I learned during my interactions with potential clients, most people feel that life insurance is an expense and not a necessity. Plus, it is not something the person buys for themselves but rather for their family – since they are dead by the time the money is collected.

In a society that values instant gratification and consumer products, life insurance is neither sexy, nor pretty. Plus, it does not taste in any way delicious, and therefore it is not an enticing product to buy. The main consequence of this fact is that a lot of people feel no urgency in having the coverage. I have had the unpleasant surprise to meet a few people who told me they didn't care what happened to them after they died; the wife was free to bury them in the backyard or burn them in the backyard – whatever she preferred. I found that disturbing not simply because it was insensitive but also because it implies that the wife should do something illegal and go to prison after they are dead. That did not speak of love to me. But what do I know?! I was raised in another country, a place where life insurance didn't even exist until the 1990's, and people still got buried – through other financing methods that didn't prove as much of a burden for the family as I have discovered during my life in the U.S.

The heartbreaking situations were those when my appointments were with people who understood the need for life insurance and wanted to get the coverage for themselves and their family but they could not qualify medically. A fact that many people don't know is that the life insurance companies don't want to accept someone who is considered a high risk due to medical conditions or a bad behavior (like multiple DUI's or convictions for felonies). I have always encouraged the people I met to protect themselves and their family at that time – when they could qualify – because tomorrow is never promised. And even if we don't die, we don't know what may happen that would make it impossible to get the coverage at a later time. The sadness came over me when I met the people who had already been diagnosed with medical conditions which made them ineligible for life insurance – I always wondered whether someone had talked to them about getting insured and they had refused.

I worked with the life insurance company for 8 years and talked about death and the devastating consequences to the surviving family every day. The only way to cope with the sad situations and the ignorance of some prospects was to quickly learn that I could not save everybody – no matter how hard I tried. All I could do was my best. All I could do is provide the information that would allow them to make an informed decision. At that point, the result was out of my hands, whether I liked it or not.

From a business perspective, I am grateful for my years with the life insurance company because it trained me to work independently and with little supervision. I have always been disciplined and got things done. This was my opportunity to prove – to myself and to anyone else who might be watching – that I could apply those lessons in business, not just in school. I embraced the motto of "lead by example" and never required from any member of my team anything that I was unwilling to do myself.

The self-employed status during my career there taught me a lot about the tax laws in the U.S. I learned about keeping my bills and receipts for tax records. And I learned that as a self-employed person I could deduct business-related expenses before paying taxes on the income I made. With over 50,000 miles on my car in the first year – while visiting the prospects I had appointments with – the tax deduction of mileage definitely came in handy.

I became an expert in life insurance but accepted the fact that I was not an expert in taxes, so I had professional tax preparers help me with the returns during my years with the life insurance company. It gave me an opportunity to ask many questions from the professionals and to learn the importance of a home office deduction, as well as the deductions for travel (daily by car, or overnight for roadtrips) and for eating out with colleagues and teammates, and also with potential clients.

This first taste of entrepreneurism from the safe harbor of self-employment taught me the importance of financial knowledge – in this case, when dealing with taxes. I learned the advantages that I now had, by comparison with the time I had spent as an employee. Even though I was making more money and working about the same number of hours (give or take), I was paying a lot less in taxes, for a very simple reason: as an employee, I got paid, paid taxes and spent the remainder; as a self-employed person I got paid, spent money for my business and paid taxes on what I had left after that. Learning how to reduce my tax liability was a great lesson, one that has served me well in the years since.

While with the life insurance company, I continued to expand my knowledge of financial matters in the new country where I now lived. I figured that I needed to know and understand what was different from what I had learned growing up, how that applied to my current situation and how I could use that information. I adopted the "leaders are readers" motto and read books on financial matters, in addition to the sales and self-development books recommended by the leaders of the company. That is how I learned there were many solutions available for the people who wanted to improve their financial situations but most of them required commitment and hard work – the primary reasons people give up on their weight loss goals, as well their financial goals. And since there are no mandatory financial education classes for adults, it is easier for most people not to bother with learning such "boring" and "scary" lessons.

I made a commitment to myself to pursue more education and eventually more professional credentials in the financial industry, after the career with the life insurance company. I liked the idea of consulting with potential clients on a variety of issues they struggled with, not just life insurance. The idea of talking to people about other insurance needs and about financial goals, and being able to offer solutions on those issues was very appealing to me; especially when I was meeting a lot of people who needed help beyond what a life insurance policy could offer.

I still remember from the early days with the life insurance company how people asked for long-term care insurance and I was unable to serve that need because the company where I worked did not have such policies. It was a little frustrating to neither be able to help the people with the products they needed nor make the money from such sales. I remember wishing I could help them, or at the very least send them to someone who could.

Unfortunately, for all the sales training we were offered as agents, we never learned how to build relationships with potential contacts who could refer us business and whom we could refer business to. The structure of the company made prospecting unneces-sary – at least for most of my tenure here, so we were not encouraged to meet people outside of the prospects the company connected us with. This was the main attraction when I joined the company – since I was fairly new to Richmond and didn't know a lot of people – but it became a hindrance later in my career.

Looking back on my entire career in the financial and insurance industry, the first step – with the life insurance company – was a good stepping stone for me. Things may have turned out differently had I started within a different setup. I'm grateful for all the lessons I learned – what to do and also what not to do – because they have formed me professionally and also helped me grow personally.

A wise man said "some people come into your life for a reason, some for a season and some for a lifetime". I can think of a few reasons this episode of my life was very important. This was a season that opened new opportunities for me and helped stir the curiosity of studying anything and everything related to money: how to make it, how to keep it and how to protect it and pass it on. I always wanted to learn more about finances – this career opened the door to that knowledge. And I walked right in.

Chapter 6: The Independence

With the lessons learned while working with the life insurance company, I was feeling more and more strongly that I wanted to build a career in the financial industry but in such a way as to be able to help clients with many of their needs, not just with the protection of life insurance. I started thinking that once my 10-year commitment was up, I would research different financial certifications and then figure out how to go about getting them and finding a company to work with. I wanted to broaden my knowledge in the field.

At the time I was aware of the differences between a captive agent (working exclusively with only one company) and an independent agent (working with a variety of companies). I was also familiar with many of the life insurance companies around the country but did not know details about brokerage companies and about which life insurance companies would want an independent agent versus a captive one. I also never seriously considered going to a different life insurance company. Looking back, I guess it can be said that I had drunk the Kool-Aid and become too attached to the company that I was already a part of. In truth, I understood that it was not all roses and rainbows but was willing to deal with the bad, because I firmly believed my work helped people and I had gotten used to the systems that the company had in place.

However, when the 7-year anniversary came along, I decided to start working on my exit strategy, partly because I needed a little distraction as I was getting burnt out, partly because my exit strategy needed time to be properly executed. I decided to rebuild my network marketing business. The plan was to work that business in parallel with the life insurance career and build it to the point where the income it generated would match the income from my full-time career. This would allow me to cover all my bills as I was looking for the next career opportunity within the financial industry without having to rush into anything.

The biggest revelation I had when I started executing this plan was the fact that recruiting for my team with the network marketing company now was very easy, and everything came to me naturally, without a great effort on my part. It was easy to ask people if they would be interested in joining my team, and my retention of the team members was very high.

I cannot say I was surprised, I can just say that I really appreciated being able to have more knowledge about how to build a business in one industry, and then applying that knowledge in a different industry with great success. Growth and promotion goals that had previously been hard to achieve were now blown out of the water, and I had no challenges maintaining the standards of the company as far as the size of the orders and the number of team members with great ease. These had all been insurmountable challenges in the past, during my first attempt at building this same business, in the direct selling industry. The best explanation that I have for the shift in my business knowledge and application of that knowledge is the change in my mindset regarding that business. If before I had always considered my direct selling venture as a side business, a source for additional cash to top off my "real" income, now this business was part of my exit strategy and it had become imperative that I succeed, so I could execute the exit strategy; otherwise the whole plan would fall apart. And that was unacceptable for me.

These principles helped me tremendously in achieving leadership goals in a short period of time. I also increased my sales, first by contacting former clients who had not ordered in a long time, and then by finding new ones during my regular daily activities while applying different prospecting techniques learned both from Avon and the insurance company. I firmly believe that for me Avon was the easiest thing to sell not just because of my belief in the products but also because of their more than 130-year brand recognition.

My plan was unfolding nicely, and I had a booming business with Avon both in personal sales as well as team size and production – with over 70 representatives in a few months and over $100,000 in team sales in the first year. Everything looked encouraging, and I firmly believed that I was on track to shift careers once my 10-year commitment came to a close. And that was true, until…

Another disruptor came in my path and I made the decision to shift course yet again. And I started over on a new path, with a new company – in the financial industry. This was a smaller company with a strong local representation and the independence that I was looking for. And most importantly for me, it was a company that covered many aspects of the financial life of a family, from paying off debt to saving for retirement and from life insurance to estate planning. When I first heard about the company, I was intrigued to find out that they were focused on explaining financial lingo to people and empowering them to take control of their personal finances by first learning what it all meant and then by acting on that knowledge. The principles that the teachings were based on came from old mentors of mine like Robert Kiyosaki and Suze Orman, as well as Dave Ramsey, whom I was not yet as familiar with.

The idea of working with people on the entire spectrum of their financial life and educating them about it, rather than just advising them on what was best for them and which course to take, appealed to me on many levels, especially because I was very interested in my own financial education in a country so completely different from my homeland.

While helping clients pay off their debt and saving for retirement, as well as setting up life insurance policies to protect them and their families, I found out I really enjoyed having different options to present as well as avenues to be able to serve people better. Though my clients were both men and women, my focus was mainly on helping women understand their finances and taking care of the family's needs. I always understood that by improving the financial knowledge of the woman in the family, the entire family benefits because she is the one who typically will be in charge when something happens to a family member: parent or sibling gets sick, she will take care of them; parent or sibling dies, she will make sure the funeral arrangements are made, and she will hold the family together through the hard times. The scary knowledge that I gathered through my interaction with many families was that even though the woman in the family is usually in charge of the moral support through tough times, she is usually not in charge of the financial support during those times. In the typical American families that I have encountered during my tenure with the life insurance company, I learned that the man is in charge of the family's finances. Once I started working with a company that gave me access to resources to change that, I made it my mission to bring women closer to the knowledge they needed to handle the family's finances together with the husband.

During the time I was working with the life insurance company, I had come across many situations where one of the spouses knew where all the important documents were, as well as what life insurance coverage the family had, while the other spouse was not even sure they had life insurance. In many instances, the one who deferred this responsibility to her spouse was the wife. This determined my decision to focus on teaching women what they need to know about the family's finances. I had already met many women who had had to deal with a family member's death or serious illness. This, correlated with the statistic showing that women live longer than men, proved to me the importance for women to learn about the financial lingo before they were put in a situation when they had to make decisions under pressure and while grieving.

This time in my career taught me about making connections and building relationships based on trust in my new home country. Coming across the ocean, one of the hardest things to adapt to was the separation from everyone I had grown up with and known all my life. After having been able to find someone to help with anything and everything I could have possibly needed, it was hard to ask my new friend, Google, for referrals for things I needed taken care of. So, I made it my mission to build a great Rolodex – I'm aware that is an outdated word, so for the young readers, this would be the people I know, like and trust. I made it my mission to know someone for everything anyone could possibly need or want, so that if my clients or friends needed help, I would be able to direct them to someone who could help to resolve their problems.

Even though the number one thing that attracted me to the career opportunity with the life insurance company was the fact that I was not responsible for prospecting (because of my personal situation at the time – still somewhat of a newcomer to the country, not yet knowing a lot of people, unfamiliar with the opportunities that would enable connecting with prospects), at this time in my career I decided to tackle the networking scene and learn about prospecting and building relationships. I discovered that I found it easy to talk to strangers and turn them into acquaintances and later on friends.

I have since read a lot of books on networking and learned how to meet people and make connections in a business environment the right way, without appearing desperate and without soliciting business all the time and to the point that it turns people off. Thinking back to my first forays into networking, I realized that I had avoided these mistakes instinctively in the beginning simply because I found them off-putting. I later learned that I had actually followed the Golden Rule: "treat others the way you want to be treated". Since I didn't enjoy talking to people who were too busy selling me their wares to listen to what I had to share, I never put others through this experience.

One of the things I missed most after my relocation had been the fact that I did not know people who could help with different needs. Therefore, when I started networking, my main goal was to fill in this void in my life, and I started with the assumption that I could be of value to any new contacts because, like me, the new contacts I made would need access to other new contacts I was making. And herein was my value: I was a conduit for these new relationships.

Only after talking to others and attending seminars and workshops on better networking techniques, did I realize that this was not a natural way to network for most people – however, for me, this was the only way it made sense. I realized that it took a while to build real relationships and there was no way to rush this time-consuming process along. I realized that my value in a business built on prospecting and relationships came from the value I could give others and from the time that I was willing and able to invest in all the relationships I was building.

As I am looking back on both of these insurance and financial businesses – one built on sale meetings with prospects that were already in the sales funnel through a highly-specialized PR department and the other built on personal relationships and a lot of prospecting – I realize that even though I was in the same industry (life insurance and financial services), I was working in different aspects of the business. Therefore, I learned how to build the business from the inside – as part of a trained sales force, following proven scripts and systems – as well as from the outside – building a large number of potential prospects for a sales funnel and then sifting through those prospects and figuring out who can and will move forward with the sales process.

The almost 4 years of experience with this brokerage firm showed me the "other side of the coin", when it comes to insurance and financial services. In my formative years in the industry, I was with a captive company – only able to market their products and services – while in the growth years I was working independently, in association with a company that offered a wider range of products and services through partnerships with multiple life insurance and financial companies.

Throughout my career in the life insurance industry, by talking to thousands of prospects and clients, and during the years as an independent agent, while building and maintaining the relationships I have developed, I learned that most people are quite visibly uncomfortable even talking about their own financial situation. When it comes to life insurance, most people I have encountered rely on benefits provided by the employer, while many of the ones who have outside policies are not exactly sure what type of coverage they provide. Therefore, I have taken it upon myself to not only explain to people what I (as a licensed professional) think fits their needs, but also educate them on how to make informed decisions, since they will affect their family's financial wellbeing.

While I always worked with both men and women as clients and team members, my main focus has shifted over the years more toward the women because I realized that I can affect more people through the women in the family, as the caretakers. Also since statistically women live longer, it is very important for them to become comfortable dealing with financial matters before their situation forces them to do it suddenly and while they are unprepared.

In the summer of 2016, I decided to put a name to my efforts and goals, and I incorporated my own company under the name Un-Broke Women LLC. The name comes from the certainty that women who want to be wealthy and leave behind their broke state, have to first become unbroke, lift themselves first to a status of not thinking like a broke person and believing in their dreams and goals, and pursuing them. Then and only then, can they even hope to achieve financial wealth and independence.

Focusing mostly on the actual tools and tactics to achieve one's financial goal, I understand however the importance of mindset in such matters. As I am an avid reader, I am in a perpetual search for books that tackle the mindset of abundance and the believe that there is enough for everyone and that getting a larger piece of the pie does mean someone else loses. I emphasize this in my workshops and one-on-one consultations, aiming to expand my clients' belief system. Henry Ford's words have been guiding me for a long time: "Whether you think you can, or you think you can't, either way, you are right."

Chapter 7: The Story Continues

As my business grew into a bigger venture, and I officially became a business owner, not only a self-employed person, I also made the decision to join a larger brokerage firm. My decision was based on logical reasons, even though there were emotional ones as well. When discussing financial woes with my clients, I always advise following the logical route, because the emotions can lead down the wrong path. Since I always practice what I preach, I knew it was time for me to do the same. Money has such a logical and mathematical explanation, yet it is very charged emotionally... And since this is at the core of my passion for teaching about money, I had to stand by the logic and not rely too much on the feelings in order to make the right decision for myself and my future. And ultimately, my feelings did confirm my logical decision.

I am also blessed with a strong sense of reality and logic, so I looked at this opportunity from a variety of angles, in order to make the best decision for the present and future of both my business and myself. Ultimately, the result was a new adventure, and a new beginning. My life is sprinkled with new beginnings! This is a beauty of making things happen and not waiting for things to happen to you. This may be a little bit of my controlling streak showing but I will not apologize. I'm very comfortable with the woman I have become – the good, the bad and the ugly parts of me. And therefore, I make sure there are no regrets for the things left behind. I have always preferred to act so I would never regret what might have been.

Even with access to more companies and products, my focus still remains on the business women who are so busy building their business that they either neglect their personal finances or they delegate it to their spouse. Since statistically we live longer, we need to know more about our personal finances because there will come a time when we will, most likely, have to deal with our money (or lack thereof) and the hardest time to do that is in a time of grief. Plus, for those business owners who may consider their business their retirement plan... well, that may not work out as they wish. The fact that you put your blood, sweat, and tears into your business doesn't mean that someone will buy it; and it certainly does not mean they would pay what you want to get. One other thing to consider in making your business sellable is the systems you have in place and the amount of work required of you in the daily operations because nobody wants to buy your job.

These lessons I learned about women in the US, and especially business and career women, are the reasons behind my passion for educating them on their financial situation. I made a commitment to myself to make sure their dreams come true and they can have the financial serenity they want and need.

Keeping all this in mind, I started a new chapter in my business life, and a new beginning, in the spring of 2016. (Funny how this is considered the season of new growth and change, and many of my ventures started in spring, including my moving to a new country.) I am more mature and I understand the rules of small business and personal finances better than when I first embarked on this ship. Even though I realized there would be a time of rebuilding and with it the challenges of a new business, I also know that this new adventure is a continuation of my journey on the same path, and therefore the learning curve is not as steep as the first time around. I'm carrying with me the lessons of all my previous experiences, and also the friendships, relationships and connections from my previous endeavors.

I heard the expression "back to square one", which doesn't have an exact equivalent in Romanian, just an equivalent (back to the start line). I have been working it out in my mind to see if it feels like this is where I was by joining a new company. I'm pretty familiar with the "new kid on the block" feeling by now, so this was not really a concern, just a puzzle to think over. And I realized that whenever I started a new venture, I would never have to start from square one, since all my experiences and skills were coming with me. With staying in the same field, all I was doing was an upgrade to my opportunity and my options, without hitting the restart button.

After so many beginnings in my life, I have learned to embrace the inherent challenges that come with the new opportunities. I have also learned that every new start builds on the experience and skills built before, so I never have to start from zero again. All this wisdom was gained through years of trial and error, through many trials and tribulations, and I remember fondly (now that I'm safely past that moment) when I was starting off, and wishing for more experience and credibility. This just proves how true the saying "be careful what you wish for..." is. Cliché as it may sound, some days now I wish for the youth from before, with the boundless energy and fearless determination in the pursuit of my goals – I still have the determination, but the energy ebbs and flows.

My life mantra is to think carefully and analyze all decisions (though not for long) and then act; and upon acting to assume responsibility for the action, so I can never regret the steps taken, and more importantly, the steps not taken. Changing the company to be affiliated with was the perfect logical decision for many reasons, though the emotional part of the decision was hard. But once the decision was made, I not only stood by it, but also received confirmation from subsequent events that the decision I had made had been the right one.

I have always relied on my intuition – some call it gut instinct – to lead me in the right direction. And it has always proven to be the best judge of the situation I needed to evaluate. Even though sometimes I had friends telling me that I had outlandish ideas, and even my husband sometimes would try to make a logical point against the way my instinct was leading me, it has never led me astray, and has always proven to be a faithful companion along the path I had chosen. This is one more reason for me to work mainly with women in my practice – since we listen more to our instincts and intuition than logic, and we make decisions that "feel" right for no apparent reason that our spouses can see, even when they may not "sound" right – at least to others.

With this new direction of my business, and with the upgrade to a higher level of professionalism and responsibility, also came an upgrade in my professional licenses and accreditations. Within 8 months, I can proudly say that I passed two licensing exams that now provide the highest standard of qualification and responsibility within the financial industry. I am a fiduciary investment advisor, meaning that my number one requirement for any recommendations made to a client is that they have to be the client's best interest. The fact that I have always conducted my business this way is now supported by the rules and laws of the industry, and its regulatory body – FINRA. This comes to illustrate that the way I say I lead my business is truly the way I do.

Studying for an exam, is always difficult and the emotions usually make it harder to focus. This is why I consider myself fortunate and blessed to be what is considered a good tester. I have always been able to focus while in the exam. I have the butterflies prior to getting to the testing center, just like everyone else. I'm happy that I can focus and center once I get set and start looking at the test material. Despite some people being amazed that I can pass tests in a language that is not my native tongue (on the first try), it never occurred to me to feel disadvantaged or ask for extra time due to a need to translate the information.

In these cases, the tests are multiple-choice, without being told whether or not you are on track to the passing score, so you cannot breathe more comfortably as you get closer to the end. And, of course, you have no idea which questions you got right and which questions you got wrong, so even if you review them, changing the answers might not be a good idea. Plus, there is always the belief that if you are not sure, you should just stick with your first choice because that was based on gut instinct. The ability to breathe more comfortably during practice tests comes from seeing the progress of the score – and this is the main thing that can throw someone off during the real test. With the passing of the time, you can get worried about the progress of the score to that point.

I'm grateful for the "elephant memory" I have. I can remember a lot of things when I need to – i.e., in front of the computer during testing. Therefore, even though, prior to studying for these tests, I was not very familiar with some of the definitions and concepts I had to study, I was able to use the information I studied and correctly answer enough questions to pass with flying colors. I never took an exam twice throughout my school years and afterward; and I had no intention to make this the first failed exam. I tackled both of these exams with the mindset that I just had to get it done and over with on the first try. I have a lot of projects going on currently, and studying twice for the same exam was not in my plans. I have always known that if I buckle down and study (while cramming works for me, I'm not relying exclusively on it), I will pass any test I work on.

Now, when I say I never fail a test, that does not mean I just show up and miraculously pass. I do study beforehand. I have to also say that I never went to an exam unprepared. I have to tell the skeptical readers about following my instinct about the way I study, and I also cram really well. I'm not sure if my method of preparing for an exam can be duplicated by others, but it certainly has served me well throughout school and some specialty certifications. There is a French expression – "la noblesse oblige" – that has always been my mantra for testing. I feel that after performing well for all the tests I ever took throughout school, college and professional accreditations, I have to maintain the standard that I have set for myself. With this in mind, I always prepare so I cannot fail.

I am aware that there are many professors who advise against cramming for an exam – I had some of them in college – and I'm not suggesting this method of studying for anyone other than myself. It has always worked for me to increase the intensity of my studying by immersing myself in the material I need to remember on a given day, the closer it gets to that day. For me it is also a matter of mindset: I attack every exam challenge with the mindset that it will be the one and only time we meet. Taking exams in fields that I had very little experience in, and a lot of interest, has been somewhat of a challenge – therefore, like any good challenge, it had to be conquered. And I won.

I tackled the Life Insurance and Annuities, and Health Insurance licensing exam at a time when my only experience in the field had been very limited and only in Romania. And then after years in the insurance field I wanted to expand my expertise into the investments arena, so I needed to acquire the necessary licenses. Under guidance from a very experienced mentor, I set out to take the Series 66 and Series 7 exams, without a lot of experience with the practical knowledge. I do believe that actually worked to my advantage: I had no preconceived ideas about what things mean or how they work, and no habits to ignore or change.

Part of my "growing up" as a business owner – since I now had the legal set up as an LLC, I decided to associate myself with a large local company, and through them with one of the largest broker-dealer in the investment industry in the world. The decision was not an easy one. Logically, it made sense because of the higher level of expertise and professionalism, plus the benefit of an experienced mentor to guide my steps as a newly licensed investment advisor. The emotional decision was a lot harder. After 4 years with a company, it was hard to break away because of a feeling of loyalty and belonging. And I was not really excited about the idea of being the new kid on the block either. But I followed the logic and my instincts and am now in a better place professionally, and a happier place personally.

Ultimately, logic prevailed, and I made the change. My heart was heavy for a while because I was leaving behind a group of friends whom I cared for and a company that I had helped grow. But subsequent events proved me right. The company I had just left went out of business shortly afterward, unexpectedly for most of my former team and associates. To me, this was even more proof that I should always trust my instincts and move in the direction they indicate because they never stir me wrong, though it may look difficult at first.

I am frequently asked about my new career, and I always explain that it is not new to me; it is actually a continuation of what I have been doing for almost 5 years now. The biggest change is the company I now work through – and the fact that I have incorporated my business and no longer operate as a sole proprietor. Both of these changes were made with the vision for bigger and better things on the horizon.

In my 15 years in the U.S., I have learned a lot about the business side of entrepreneurial endeavors and I'm applying my knowledge to improve the business I'm building, in the same way I would advise any client to do for their own business; always practicing what I preach.

In this new adventure (or on this new path of my adventure), I'm looking at more opportunities that are opening up to me, and I make sure I am available and my hands are ready to receive. I'm just as dedicated as ever to the improvement of financial understanding and education for women – especially business women and women who are building a successful career in the corporate world. I have met too many who are so focused in one area, that they almost run away from their personal finances.

In conversations with business owners, I'm always intrigued by the passion they have in whatever they are doing (or making) in their business – such as baking, plumbing, coaching, teaching – but I'm also amazed that they have no desire to understand the business aspect of their business.

Most business owners don't spend a lot of time doing back office work, especially the part that is directly related to money. And even worse, they also delegate their personal finances to someone else, most frequently the spouse.

Chapter 8: My Money Story

(from my interview on Money Mondays Radio Show)

1. What is your biggest money accomplishment?

I think that my biggest money accomplishment is the fact that I have been able to be self-employed for over 10 years now in my adoptive country; and just being able to maintain that, and not having had to depend on anyone for a paycheck, represents an accomplishment that I'm proud of. And for me coming from a background within a blue-collar family that always depended on a paycheck, I think that is a major accomplishment. I am able to sustain my lifestyle and do the things that I want to do and not really depend on a 9 to 5 or a regular steady paycheck. Once I learned about entrepreneurial ventures and the way they can work in the U.S., building my own business became a no-brainer. I'm happy to see the fruits of my labor and to wake up every morning knowing that I'm one step closer to my goals and dreams.

2. What is a money memory from childhood that comes to your mind right now?

Well, growing up, my parents were, like I said, blue-collar. So, they went to work and brought home a paycheck. Back then it actually used to be cash. My mom's job was to actually give out the wages in her department within the plant. Sometimes she would bring home new bills because since she was giving out the wages, she tried to put those to the side. So, she would take the money I had saved and trade it for new, crispier bills, better looking, prettier ones than I had at that time. And, for me, that was really cool because I liked the new money. Actually, to this day, I like the new bills that have no creases, and I'm still inclined to save them.

So, if I would get any new bills – let's say instead of what in the U.S. would be five $20 bills, I would get one $100 bill – it would help me save money. I always had some cash stashed somewhere because I liked the feel of new money and I didn't want to part with it. The newer and the bigger the bill, the better, because I would hold on to it the longest and I would not feel compelled to spend it on trivial things. I guess you could say this was how I learned to save.

3. What is your biggest money challenge? (currently or ever) – if past, how did you overcome it?

For me, the biggest thing was coming here (to the U.S.) and having to figure out how things are done in this country. Before coming to the U.S., I didn't even know what a credit card was. I knew what a mortgage was only because we had one of those when I was growing up (though a lot different set up than here), but not what a credit card was. I didn't know how those interest rates can cripple your finances for many, many years. So, I learned those lessons: some of them the hard way, some of them from other people. But it was a good lesson to understand all of that.

My husband (the one I married before coming here, and whom I'm still married to) is of the opinion that if he didn't have enough money to pay it off, he would not buy it. And when I first arrived in the U.S. we needed reliable cars – or at least one, since at the time I was not driving. So, we got some clunkers for cars because he didn't want to have monthly car payments. When I finally decided that was not going to work for me anymore, I had to learn how car financing worked, because he never needed it. So, I had to learn on my own.

We had 7 cars in my first 2 years in the U.S., and that was not because we had a lot of money and we wanted to have 7 cars, but because they were dying. At the time my husband was driving me everywhere. Based on that experience, when I started driving myself, and while having a career that required transportation because of a lot of field work, plus being a woman driving mostly by myself, I had to have a reliable car. I had to have a car that would not die on the side of the road. That was a big one for me. From my need for reliable transportation, I learned a lot about credit purchases, credit score and credit history. It was quite stressful at the time but also very educational for someone who had no experience with the U.S. credit system.

4. Share a money lesson you guide yourself by – your money mantra or belief.

The most significant thing is to make sure that I have some money left at the end of the month. This way I know I'm OK at the beginning of the month. And the reason I'm saying this is because I'm self-employed, and I have to make sure that my months run together smoothly. I don't know when the next check is coming, so I have to make sure that I have enough money for the next bill. That way, when I get my next paycheck, I have enough for the next bill. So that is my plan. As someone who had been working on commission for many years now, the planning from one check to the next is a little different from the employees with a predetermined amount coming to their bank account every week or every other week.

I would not say I'm great at budgeting every dollar, but I became really good at establishing priorities and making sure the income went toward necessary expenses before going to unimportant things. Fluctuations in income (as all entrepreneurs can relate to) taught me to classify my expenses in 3 categories: fixed, flexible and discretionary. And this is how I managed my finances.

> 5. *If money were no object, what would your perfect day look like?*

Well, I'm an animal lover, so I would probably spend it with cats. I know that is not expensive, so it is not about the money, but that is what I would enjoy. I also like traveling so if money were no object, I would travel a lot more than I do now – and I already travel quite a bit. And if money really were no object and I had all the money I needed, I would probably take my cats with me on trips – which would be really interesting.

I would also go back to Florida and visit the Big Cat Rescue, which is a sanctuary for big cats. And if I could have all the money that I wanted on a regular basis, and not just as a onetime lump sum but as cashflow, I would like to be able to donate to them enough to keep a tiger there. When I was there I learned that it takes about $10,000 per year just to feed the tiger – it doesn't include housing, medicine, surgeries or whatever they might need. So, I would like to literally adopt a tiger there – just feed that tiger for the rest of his or her life.

Being able to help animals, especially cats big and small, and be a voice for them to enact changes in legislature and people's behavior is my WHY for working on my business to grow it and make it a financial success.

6. Share a goal that you achieved that had a price tag.

In 2015 I bought a brand-new car. I really needed it because my old one, even though it was still good and working, was kind of old by then. And I was able to buy the car paying it off in cash. That was really awesome because I don't have to worry about a car note. I have a new car that hasn't needed (thank God) any repairs. And probably won't need any for a long time. I'm a big fan of Corollas. I'm still in the same brand family, nothing fancy. But it is a car that I know I can rely on to take me where I need to go – and I do drive a lot. So, I like to know that wherever I need to get, I can get there and I won't risk dying on the side of the road because of the car failing.

Achieving this goal was great not for flashy reasons and vanity but for practical reasons and because I wanted to practice what I preach. The new car was a necessity; a luxury vehicle was not. So, I took care of what was necessary in setting and achieving my goal.

For those listeners who want to get a car and cannot pay for it in cash and will have a 5- or 6-year loan, my advice to help pay that faster is to wait a little bit if you can. Look at your credit score and fix whatever you can on your credit report to raise your credit score – if it is not an emergency. If it is an emergency, then, of course, you go ahead and buy. If you don't need to worry about your credit score, then you can buy. But most people have little bumps and bruises on their credit report. Fix your credit report as much as possible before committing to a purchase with a payment whose size is determined by your credit score. The higher you can get your credit score, the lower your interest and your monthly payments will be.

Once you get the car, pay a little extra each month (however much you can, without putting yourself in a bind). My first car that I financed, the car I traded in last year, I had a 5-year loan on it. I wanted to pay a little more; so, I actually didn't take the whole 5 years on it. It feels really great not to have a car payment. That is why, though I wanted a new car, I was really determined not to get a new loan, because I knew how good it felt not to have a payment. So, if you can, and there is a way to ask them to put the extra toward the principal, that is what you want to do – make sure that principal goes down.

7. If you could double your income, what would you do with the extra money?

At this point, if I doubled my income I think that I'd probably save some of that toward purchasing my dream home. We do own the house where we live, but it is not the dream home. It is the house that we got, and we are glad to have it. It would be great to have a dream home at this time because I don't want to be retired and cut grass and do maintenance, so by then, I would probably be ready to downsize. Therefore, if I can hurry up and get my dream home now, I can enjoy it for some years until that time comes. That would probably be what I would do with the extra money. And, of course, save some for later, because I'm always planning for my retirement.

I need to point out that I don't see retirement as a vegetative state – posing as a couch potato – but as a time when I work because I want to, and not because I have to. I also see retirement as a time when I focus more on giving back – through the charities that I support, and working on changing the world. Just heard the phrase "going from success to significance" recently and it spoke to me; it suggests a time when I would focus exclusively on helping the community, and most of all, the animals I love – without tracking numbers (activity and revenue) for my business.

8. What is the one thing you wish you knew when you were 21?

At 21 I graduated from college back in Romania, so I really had no idea what I wanted to do with my life, other than start a career in the travel industry. I started working for a travel agency that was owned by somebody that I didn't really respect a lot because he didn't seem to know what he was doing within the agency. If I could look back from where I am now and talk to myself back then, I would say "Don't worry about working for these people, because that is not what you are going to do for the rest of your life, so you don't really need this kind of experience." But it is funny how we go to school… and actually my degree is in tourism – and I really wanted to work in travel agencies. My goal was to travel to different places and know more about places where I can tell people to travel. And once I moved to the U.S., even though I'm still traveling, I don't do that for a living. So, it is funny that I just am on a totally different career path.

I would probably say that it is best to learn as much as you can about the business side of whatever business you are in.

Even if it is not your own, don't learn just how to do whatever your job is. Learn how the business is run because if at any point you want to start your own business, that is the number one thing that you are going to use. That is the most important knowledge: be an apprentice of the business, not just the craft. You can then use the knowledge with whatever craft you develop later.

A lot of people fail in their businesses due to not knowing the business aspect, not because they are not good at whatever their business is. If you are a fantastic baker, you may have the best cupcakes or the best cakes ever, but if you don't know how to run a business, you can still go bankrupt. Or if you are a good plumber, it doesn't mean you know how to run a business. So that is probably what I would tell myself: "Learn as much as possible about running the business, not just the activity you are responsible for."

9. *What advice would you give a woman just starting her business/career?*

If she hasn't started the business yet, I would say "Talk to somebody who is in the same business you are interested starting, someone who is already successful in that field, someone you admire and respect. And ask them if you can hang out with them, help them around their office or anywhere in their company and learn how things are run. Offer to be an unpaid intern and see what you can soak up." You don't have to do it forever. And don't look at it like you are just slave labor and you have to work for free and they don't pay you. But look at it as an opportunity to learn how the business is run. This is an opportunity to learn for free, whereas in college you have to pay for the information. Take advantage of this free education opportunity.

Like I said, you may be the best baker but you have to have some business acumen. And really the only way to learn it is by soaking up from somebody else who is great at it. Because you can read books and go to school, and the professors can tell you, but ultimately, they are just professors, it is not like they have businesses – some might, but most don't.

So, if you talk to whoever you are working with, find a mentor that can guide you. Look for the person that you want to be when you grow up. Find that person, and then try to hang out with them as soon as possible and for as long as possible. Because that will help you learn a lot about how to achieve what they have already achieved. It is an opportunity to learn from the best.

   10. *If you could spend 3 days with a millionaire/ billionaire, who would that be and why?*

One of my favorite people is Jon Bon Jovi – I really love his music. I'm not sure if he is really a multimillionaire (many times over) but I know he is very successful and I would love to spend some time with him and see how he runs his companies. If I could hang out with him for 3 days, I think I would learn a lot because it is not just about the fact that he can sing – which he can. Ladies, I hope you agree with me! But he also does have a great business mind.

I was watching a documentary, and he was calling somebody about setting up a meeting, and they were giving him the runaround. And he said "I am the CEO of a multimillion dollar corporation, I demand that we do this or otherwise I don't care; I'm not interested." And at that point I realized that he is absolutely right; he does run a multimillion dollar corporation.

So, I would love to learn something from him. I believe he knows what he is doing.

Another great point I still remember from the same documentary is him saying "this is not a democracy" – when referring to the Bon Jovi company. I took to heart the idea that someone has to make the executive decisions and take responsibility for the outcomes.

Chapter 9: The Lessons

I want to focus on listing the most important lessons I have learned so far, regarding money, in this chapter. I hope my readers will come back to this part of the book every time they have a question or are not sure about a money situation that arises in their life. I will make it easy for everyone to find the answer they are looking for, right here.

O **My favorite methods of saving painlessly**

The reason why most people don't save is that they decide to save the money they have left after paying the bills and spending on both needs and wants. The majority of months, they don't have anything left after spending on things they want – even though sometimes they mask wants as needs.

Most financial gurus will advise to "pay yourself first" and put 10% of the money you get paid into savings; and then live on the rest, to cover both needs and wants. They are correct in explaining that everyone saving by this method will figure out ways for the money to be enough.

Depending on how you get the income, you can have an automatic deposit straight from the paycheck, or an automatic transfer from the checking account on preset days. If you get commissions, you may consider a percentage of income; whereas, if you get a fixed salary, you may want to designate a set amount.

O **The best place for your savings account**

The strategies that always worked for me were to have a savings account at a bank a little out of the way, where I don't go very often, or to use an online bank – again one that I don't use on a regular basis.

The one trick that has always helped me to keep the money in savings, is to not look at the money too often. Out of sight, out of mind concept at its best!

O SMART goals and why they are important

The SMART acronym is very popular today and many people use it when setting their goals. I will just emphasize that I guide myself by the rules of SMART (Specific, Measurable, Attainable, Relevant, Timebound) because it feeds the needs of my competitive nature. I like tracking the progress of my work toward achieving the goals I set, and I find that vague goals get lost along the way. Therefore, I never set goals like "lose weight", "make more money", "be happy" – there is no quantifiable way for me to figure out whether or not I achieved that goal. More money may mean an extra $100 per month, or increasing my income 10 times. But unless that detail is specified, there is no way for me to know that I reached the goal I set, since even an extra dollar earned represents more money.

My favorite definition for goals is "a goal is a dream with a deadline". With that in mind, I always want to reach the destination at a specific time. If I only want to get somewhere eventually, then any day, any month, any year will do; and in that case, there may not be any progress for a long time, because there is no urgency to reach the goal. This can become demoralizing on the one hand, and encourages procrastination on the other hand. Especially when it comes to finances, I am a big proponent of timelines. Money goals are sometimes scary for people, so any excuse to procrastinate will be taken up.

O What is a mutual fund?

Technical definitions aside, a mutual fund is a company that owns stock in many other companies – it may have a variety of companies, or only in a sector. The mutual fund company then issues its own stock and sells it; therefore, the people who buy mutual fund stock own little pieces of stock in the companies owned by the fund.

There are many different mutual funds available and not all of them are created equal. Some have managers, others are indexes – track the market. The charges vary based on the type of fund. When picking a fund, it is best to talk to a licensed financial adviser who can give you the best options for your situation, considering your risk tolerance.

Mutual funds are best known for their use in 401K plans – retirement plans offered by employers in the private sector.

O How do you figure out what is the best life insurance for your needs?

There are multiple types of life insurance available, and mainly they fit into 2 categories: term and whole life. The term lasts for some years, while the whole life lasts until age 100 or 120 – depending on the company.

Most people believe they lose the protection at the end of the term; in fact, most of the term life insurance is guaranteed renewable and convertible. It sounds more complicated than it is. It means that you can renew the coverage at the end of the term without answering medical questions. It can also be converted into a whole life policy anytime during the term, or just before expiration – also without answering medical questions.

O How much life insurance do you need?

There are 2 ways to figure out the amount of protection necessary: the expenses the family needs to cover when someone dies, and the value of the income the person would have earned had they lived. The first method is more popular.

The best-known way of calculating need for coverage is the DIME method. It stands for Debt (how much debt the family has to pay off), Income (how much money would have been earned until the youngest child turns 18), Mortgage (balance on the mortgage for the family home), and Education (cost for college for all children).

O What is the best way to pay off all your debt?

There are 2 ways to tackle debt, each with its pros and cons. One is based on paying the highest interest first, and the other one is based on paying the lowest balance first (known as the snowball effect).

They are both efficient and can be followed by anyone. The challenge is that we are humans, and we naturally procrastinate, and we also naturally get side-tracked even when we are working on the project. Therefore, when making the decision on which way works best for you, the most important to keep in mind is your personality and your motivation.

If you know you can stay focused, and if you want to pay as little as possible in interest, the "highest interest first" method may be your best choice. For the rest of us however, the most likely to succeed may be the "lowest balance first" method. The reason is the increased motivation once a debt is paid off.

Either way you decide to tackle your debt, it is important to keep working on it and never give up. The best approach is to pay the minimum required on all credit cards and other loans, except for the one you are working on at the time – whether that is the lowest balance or the highest interest. On that one, you want to put as much money as you can, in order to pay it off as soon as possible.

The monthly payments should stay fixed (or increase if possible – if you want to pay everything off faster). Once a card is paid off, all the money that was going on it should be redirected to the next debt, thus keeping the monthly at the same amount but always increasing the payment on one debt until it is paid off.

O W2 vs 1099 – advantages for the self-employed

The majority of Americans who are in their working years work for an employer and receive a for W2 at the end of the year showing them how much they have earned, and this is what they use to file their taxes. Most of them are happy to get a refund, and not have a balance to pay. This is probably the best picture of the lack of financial education in the U.S. Most Americans are happy to lend the government their hard-earned money during the year, and then get it back the following year, without getting paid any interest for that loan.

I know it is hard to come up with money to pay off a balance owed, and I have learned since I have been in the U.S. that the IRS is the worst creditor that one can ask for. There is no way to get out of paying them. So, I am not advocating owing the IRS. Ideally, you should break even and neither have to pay, nor receive any money by April 15th. However, the ideal situation hardly ever happens. The best-case scenario is to come as close as possible to the tax liability through the withholdings during the year.

For the independent contractors and the self-employed, the year-end summary of their income shows in a form 1099. This usually includes their gross income, without any taxes withheld – unless they paid quarterly estimated taxes throughout the year. Since there is no employer, the contractors are directly responsible for their tax liability.

I have learned that many Americans are uncomfortable with the status of self-employed especially due to the responsibility for the income tax. Though no different from the tax of the employee, the fact that no one else makes the arrangements and sets up the withholding scares some people. The truth is that a person who earns their income on a 1099 will have a lower tax liability than a person with a W2 – for the same amount of gross income.

The main difference is in the total amount that is taxed. While the employee gets paid the gross salary, pays taxes and then lives off the net income left, the self-employed gets paid the gross income, pays any business expenses, then pays taxes and lives off the net profit left. Those business-related expenses result in great savings from the tax liability, plus they lead to a growth of the business in many cases, which in turn means more income. Whereas, the employee is not in control of any pay-raises.

O Retirement plans: Traditional vs Roth

The Baby Boomer generation and the generations before them were used to pension plans set up by the employer they had been loyal to for 20 or 30 years. The Gen Xers and Millennials don't have those options. There are hardly any employers, beside the state and federal government that pay any pensions based on years worked with the company. What started as a supplement for the pension – the 401K – is quickly becoming the only source or retirement income from employment. And with the Social Security amount insufficient to live on, the 401K is even more essential to peace of mind.

IRAs are the other personal retirement income available to Americans who have earned income. Both the IRA and the 401K are available in pre-tax and after-tax form. The Traditional plans are funded with money from the gross income, before paying taxes on that money. Taxes are paid on the amount withdrawn in retirement as it comes out. By contrast, the Roth plans are funded with after-tax money – from the net income. The main advantage is that all the money withdrawn in retirement is tax-free.

Most accountants will recommend the Traditional IRAs because of the savings to the tax liability for the year the contributions are made. This may be the best plan for many people but not everyone. So, the best thing to do is to consult an expert before making decisions, and not apply a cookie-cutter method.

One question to consider when figuring out the best course of action is: "Do you want to pay taxes on the seed going into the ground or on the crops you will harvest?" I must say there is no universally right or wrong answer here; the only thing that matters is YOU – your personal situation, your preference, your priorities, your decisions.

O Standards: Suitability vs Fiduciary

When working with a financial adviser on your personal investment portfolio – and on the bigger picture of your personal finances – there are 2 standards that you need to be aware of, that they are bound by when it comes to how they operate for their clients.

The first one is the suitability standard: this is for the advisers who have licenses mainly in Series 6 and Series 63, and most of them work with financial companies directly.

The second one is the fiduciary standard: this is for the advisers who have licenses in Series 65, Series 66 and/or Series 7, and most of them work independently or through brokerage firms.

While the first category includes a lot of advisers who are captive, meaning that most or all of the products they offer come from one company, the second category is comprised of individuals who are not affiliated with a particular company, and have access to many different ones while also not being beholden to any one of them in particular.

The second major difference between these 2 categories is the obligation to look after the best interest of the clients. The fiduciary advisers must always put the best interest of the client first, while the advisers who have to adhere to the suitability standard must only make sure they don't give any advice that can harm the client, only advice considered suitable.

As with all the other decisions you have to make regarding your finances, there is no one perfect choice for everyone. We all have different situations, risk tolerance and needs. This is why it is always the best idea to have a private consultation with a specialist that can take one's personal situation into account before making recommendations.

Chapter 10: EPILOGUE

For now, here is the pause button in my story. This book ends here though my story continues. Writing my story has been a wonderful experience, filled with pleasure (for the opportunity to share my knowledge and experiences), honor (for the feelings that my story will bring to surface in the readers) and wonder (I'm humbled to be important and interesting enough to have something of value to share).

I have learned a lot about the laws and rules governing the finances in America. In a true chicken and egg dilemma, I could not tell for sure if I wanted to learn about money because I came here or if I came here because I was already on a path to learn as much as I could about money. Whatever came first, guided me on the path I'm walking right now. And
I feel blessed to have found my purpose in working with others (mostly women, but also a few good men) to help them walk the path of understanding their finances and building their own financial serenity.

My independence – in mind, work and finances – has always been very important to me. I have always made swift decisions but also thinking about them long enough to make sure I would not feel I made the wrong choice. I always conducted myself based on the principle that it is better to do something rather than later regret not doing it. Through my experiences in working with many people, I learned to appreciate the blessing it is to have a decisive mind and not suffer from analysis paralysis.

I decided to publish this book with the hope that my readers will find inspiration for the achievement of their dreams and also knowledge that will help them in their endeavors. I always made sure in everything I did that I would be proud of my accomplishments but not with vanity; it has always been about proving to myself (first of all) that I CAN. And then let the joy of reaching my goals seep into my mind.

This book started as an exercise in consistency: I wanted to challenge myself to writing on a regular basis. And what better topics to write about than my life story and the money lessons I learned along the way – a.k.a. my money story?! It was a trip down memory lane for me at times and a great review of different lessons that I learned while dealing with personal finances in a foreign land.

I have to admit that even though it was challenging at times, it was also a joyful experience and I also had an opportunity to learn a few things myself during this book journey. There is a saying that "we all have a book inside us" – I guess this is my way of proving that the saying is true. When I decided to write, the main reason was to build the discipline to keep writing; the decision to publish my book came only afterward. I made this decision with the hope that my readers will connect with parts of the story and will learn something that can serve them in improving their financial life.

There were so many instances throughout my life when I felt that I started over – again and again – that I learned not to be averse to change and embrace it. I will never say that change is easy, I will only say that fighting it is not the answer. The idea of going with the tide might seem like an easy way out – and sometimes it is just that. However, once I made a decision to move on – from a place, a job or a situation – I assumed responsibility for the decision and then embraced the changes that came from the move. I first created the tide, then I went with it. And in letting this book see the light of day, I hope that many women will be inspired to change the path they are on, if that path does not take them to the fulfillment of their dreams. And for those who are already on the way to achieving their goals and dreams, I hope this book will be the encouragement that they need to get over the hurdles, and to hang on, just one more day, and one more day… until they reach their destination.

For my readers who don't like where they are in their financial life, the answer is not to ignore the situation, or avoid thinking about it. The solution is to take inventory of the situation – the good, the bad and the ugly – and then figure out where you want to be, what changes you want to make. Once you have a direction, you build your plan and start heading toward your goal. I know it sounds simple, and that's because it really is. We have a tendency to complicate things by overthinking.
Now, even though it is simple, I'm not saying it is easy. It takes commitment and perseverance, and most of all time. We all have to be committed to putting in the time and the effort in order to achieve our goals, and the financial goals are no different from career or personal goals. I want to be a cheerleader for all my readers who find the strength to cross the finish line and live the life of their dreams.

I hope that every one of you will take an idea or a suggestion from the book as inspiration, or maybe even as proof that you can achieve your dreams. By reading about my life and my work, you can figure out the steps you need to take toward achieving your dreams. I am not where I want to be – yet – but

I'm heading in the right direction, and I know I will get there. Someone whom I respect greatly once told me that it is better to head slowly in the right direction than head fast in the wrong direction. If this statement just made you say "DUH", give it another read and think on it. If you are in a hurry to move in a direction, how do you know it is a right one?

I have always been a very strong-willed and decisive person, but this lesson makes me take a deep breath before making important decisions in my life, so that I make sure I head in the right direction. Sometimes, I must confess, things are not going the way I want, or even with the speed that I want. And as I already said, patience is not one of my virtues. That is definitely the biggest struggle I have: sometimes I just need to let go and release the control. Sometimes things will just happen, once I place the proper mechanism in motion. However, waiting is sometimes the hardest thing for me to do. And I understand that many people feel the same way. I hope this gives you the confidence in your strengths and skills, because we are all the sum of our qualities (good and not so good) and we need to learn to use them all.

In a world where instant gratification is what rules most people, it is hard to hear from yet another financial professional that you need to be patient, delay gratification and build your wealth a little at a time. Therefore, even though that is the sensible thing to do, I will not ask you to do that. I illustrated my challenges as a new American so that everyone can learn a lesson from the things I struggled with and from the challenges I had to overcome. Maybe you can use the knowledge to accelerate the building of your wealth by applying some of the lessons.

If you found something of value, please share this book with a friend, or give them this gift. You may change someone's life and earn their gratitude. And my mission will be accomplished. The ripple effect will move a lot of people closer to their financial goals. My dream is to be able to guide 1 million women toward financial freedom, through working 1on-1 with them, in workshops and seminars across the country as well as by sharing my story on my podcast and in this book. If you feel so inclined, please join me in my mission by telling a friend about this book or even giving it to her as a gift. It may be her first step toward financial serenity.

Reminiscing the money stories in my life was bitter-sweet. Remembering childhood memories and people very dear to me who are no longer in my life, I relived some very pleasant times – worry-free and full of the certainty that I could be and do anything. While I was reminiscing the first months of my life in the U.S., I could still relive the powerless feeling of insecurity because of the lack of knowledge regarding the way things are done in another country, as well as lack of connections with people who may be able to assist with the things I needed. Marrying someone whose best friend was Yahoo (Google's older and not so popular brother) made the transition even bumpier – the difference between what I grew up with and what I had to adjust to was like night and day.

Even though relocating across the Atlantic and starting a life without family support and without any friends nearby, is the hardest thing I have ever done, I always recommend that Americans should go live in other countries – at least for a few weeks or a few months – to experience other cultures and become more appreciative of what they have. Being grateful for what one has makes us less likely to complain about minor inconveniences, such as slow internet connection or the power being out for a couple of hours due to a storm. It is the best way that I found to cure entitlement and to experience gratitude daily.

When relocating to a new country by myself, I always consider myself blessed to have the strength to build my life relying on my own inner power to overcome all the challenges I have encountered. I have become stronger for it, and it has raised my level of awareness for the grit and determination I am capable of, when faced with challenges and when I want to achieve goals I set for myself.

I often read stories of people who overcome adversity – may it be physical or mental challenges – to become great athletes, or very successful business people. One of the recurring conclusions in these stories is that their greatness comes from the adversity they have to face. Should that obstacle not have been in their life, neither would their accomplishments been as great. This always makes me reflect on how far I have come along my own journey and how I have had to change and grow both personally and professionally in order for that journey to even be possible. Given the same timeline and the support of my parents while still living in Romania with them (in the same house, according to tradition and financial possibilities), I probably would not have come as far financially, nor would I have built the level of independence I now have. We always have a tendency to take the easy road; and I would have been no exception, had I stayed in the environment that was familiar to me.

However, I decided to take the challenge and find out what I can do for myself. I think it was a little bit of the feeling the child of someone famous gets when they want to step out of their parent's shadow. Not that my father is famous, but he wanted to be the one who found me a job and helped me get it, and also build my career in that company. I would have worked in the same company with him and been surrounded by co-workers who all knew I was his daughter. Though this may sound appealing to some people, I have never been accused of taking the easy road. Even though his connections got me the first job after college by granting me an interview, all the other subsequent ones came strictly through my efforts. Once I relocated across the Atlantic, I was way too far for my father's influence. This was also a lesson for me in the power of connections, since I acutely felt their lack. I guess this is best explained by the saying that "you don't appreciate what you have till it's gone."

Even 15 years later I remember the feelings of frustration and powerlessness during the first years when I didn't have the connections to help with different issues that I had to deal with. This happened because I had to trust on my husband's limited network of friends and family in order to get tasks done. It was not a great feeling, so I resolved to remedy the problem. I turned that lack of connections into a goal to make lots of connections. And today I can proudly say that is a goal I have achieved many times over.

I made it my mission to meet new people with every opportunity and then to develop the relationships. It was never a matter of need, nor of taking advantage of these relationships; it was simply derived from my need to have the resources available when I needed them and not depend on one other person – even when that person was my husband.

To this day I diligently work on extending my network of professional people and look for meaningful connections. It is something I enjoy, and my first focus is on delivering value to all new acquaintances. The joy and fulfillment I feel from building relationships with professional women have fueled my drive to help women with building the wealth they need and want for their financial serenity.

Someone told me recently that I had changed a lot in the few years she had known me. It was a great compliment and I received it as such, with gratitude and humility. I also thought about the time, effort and perseverance I put into achieving the result she had remarked on. The reason I'm sharing this is not to brag but to help my readers understand that all that you put your mind to can be achieved; you only have to be committed to working on it. This is indeed not easy, but it is simple – for all you have to do is figure out your plan and work it. And herein lies the difficulty.

I'm excited to share my story with you, my readers, and I do hope you will take a few seconds to let me know what you think about the book. I hope I can help people who have come to the United States from other countries, just like me, as well as people who lived here their entire life but maybe didn't have to deal with some of the things I mentioned and therefore never needed to know how to. I am committed to helping women grow their wealth, just as I was helped by the femtors I found in the books, in the seminars and in the organizations that shaped my life and career.

While reflecting on the people who inspired me to reach my goals, I understand that other women who are struggling on their path may find inspiration in learning from women they can relate to and who may have conquered some of the same obstacles. I hope I am such a person for some of my readers and I want to promise the rest that I will work on bringing you more stories of women who are walking on their path to financial serenity. Stay tuned…

Thank you for reading my story. I hope to be able to celebrate your victories and your arrival in the land of financial serenity. I like to think I helped a little, and would like to toast your achievement!

WARNING:

The following chapter is NOT for the faint of heart.

I shared some truths that might hurt tender feelings.

Please DO NOT turn the page if you are not ready for some real talk.

Chapter 11: Suck It Up, Buttercup!

PS. This chapter is not for the faint of heart!

When I first made the decision to move to the U.S., I imagined things in a very different light. It's not that I wore pink colored glasses, and I really didn't think I was naïve… it was all due to the image that the Romanians (and possibly other people) have of the U.S. and the Americans. In truth, my new country reminds me of my native country more than I ever cared to be reminded.

Some of the things I want to share in this chapter are not money lessons directly, however, they can impact your wealth – sometimes more than you would realize. This chapter is a way for me to release some tensions and frustrations but I'm also writing it because I think some of the points I'm making need to be heard by the people. At the time of this writing, I'm not sure what the final copy will look like, so I will apologize in advance if anyone is offended by what they are reading. If you reached this point, you probably have passed by a couple of warning signs, so please let this be the last warning – please do not proceed with reading the words on the following pages if your sensibilities might be offended by unvarnished truths seen through the eyes of an immigrant! I hope the money lessons I shared throughout the book will be useful and serve you well in building your financial freedom – if that is your ultimate goal – or at least a life with no money worries. The next few pages are for the people who want to know more about things hidden in plain sight, and things they might miss just because "this is how we have always done things here". If someone is inclined to act on this newfound knowledge, then we will all benefit from it. Otherwise, just use it as food for thought... it may serve you well in your pursuit of the American dream. And remember: if you are offended, this is not for you!

Lesson 1: DELAYED GRATIFICATION

I grew up in a household without a microwave and in a country without credit cards. So, I never had the option of buying anything and everything I wanted on the spot and then paying later. For anything that cost more than the money I had in my piggy bank – literally a piggy bank (or an envelope), not a bank account – I had to save the money until I accumulated the entire amount and then purchase it. And that was the normal way back then, so it was OK not to make impulse decisions to buy stuff that I didn't really want.

This was the best way to make sure that when I decided to spend money on something, it would be something I really wanted and that I was going to use, and enjoy. I was not even familiar with the expression "immediate gratification" because I never had that option. In fact, I only heard about delayed gratification in the U.S., while working in financial services. Since we never had the option to impulse buy and have immediate gratification, we were never taught that delayed gratification was better. Well, things may be different now in Romania as well, I cannot speak for that. Since I wasn't part of the microwave generation, I can only speak for what is known as Gen X in Romania.

There is debt in adulthood in Romania but that is for major purchases like a home or a car. I had never heard of buying clothes or food on credit before I came to the U.S. I never met people who lived beyond their means growing up because nobody had an opportunity to do so even if they had any inclination to. After having worked in the financial industry for years, I am inclined to agree with the financial gurus who advocate for the cash method of spending instead of using the plastic. In my childhood and early adulthood, I learned to budget because all the cash available was all the money available for the month. No bank would let you buy on credit and therefore live beyond your means. You had to expand your means if you wanted to increase your spending.

Lesson 2: WORK FOR IT!

The words "entitlement mentality" were never part of my vocabulary growing up. And this is not just because I was raised to know better than to think that someone owed me something for simply existing. The fact is, this expression does not even exist in the Romanian language. Yes, it can be translated but as an explanation, not as an expression like it is in the English language. I do understand the meaning but never heard this expression before coming to the U.S., even though I learned English back in Romania and read a lot of British books, and also spent time in England. I find this thought fascinating. I'm not saying that there are no people with entitlement mentality in Romania; I'm only saying that there is no common expression for this concept.

I cannot verify this idea but I believe it may not be as common a concept and that is why the expression was never developed. We say that this type of people feel that they are entitled, or it is owed to them. While that is a pretty close

103

equivalent, this "phenomenon" was never elevated to mentality status in Romanian.

I was blessed to be raised in a family that instilled in me the value of hard work rather than just feeling the Universe owed me something because I was such a special person and graced everyone with my presence. Instead of the "ask and you shall receive" method, I was taught the "work hard and you shall get" method. I also always had an independent streak a mile wide, so I usually preferred to figure out how to do things, rather than ask others to do them for me. I'm still puzzled by the fact that people are surprised here in Virginia when I figure out how to do certain things and how to get over certain hurdles in order to achieve the desired results. To me, that is just normal.

I guess the bureaucracy that I had to deal with during my early adult years trained me well not to ask for help unless and until I worked on the project myself, and only if there is no way to get it done without help. The main examples that come to mind are the exams I took for my professional credentials and the navigation of the immigration process upon coming to the U.S. I'm not saying it was a piece of cake, but I will say that it wasn't scary enough for me to require help from professionals in the field. Puzzles always fascinated me, so I took these challenges as puzzles to be solved.

Lesson 3: OH, THE SCHOOLS…

Growing up with public schools as the only option for education before college, it never occurred to me that there was a way to avoid going to school because the curriculum does not cover the information at a level that satisfies the parents. Homeschooling was indeed a foreign concept.

During the first few months in the U.S. I found out that the information taught in schools is a lower-class level than what I remembered from my school years back home. It is true that unfortunately, the school system in Romania is of a poorer quality now compared to what it was.

The most surprising for me was the lack of access to further information in school. Yes, with the internet, children have access to more information now than ever, and more books have been written than there were 20 years ago. The advances in all fields move now exponentially faster than ever in history. The puzzling thing for me is the fact that in order to pursue additional information, one has to go outside of what is given in the curriculum and study on their own. Not that this is a problem, as real progress is made when people push past their comfort zone and study beyond what is required. Based on what I have observed from current students' behavior, it is not likely for most of them to pursue knowledge beyond the school requirements.

I have come across many parents who are literally studying with their children because some of the projects the students are required to do are beyond their comprehension and level of accumulated knowledge up to that grade. For someone coming from a system designed to provide a lot of information so that the students can learn, should they be inclined to do so, it is puzzling to see such a discrepancy between different school levels. And with this, homeschooling one's children becomes ever more appealing, especially for the opportunity to raise the level of knowledge required at each grade level.

Lesson 4: FAMILY VALUES

This is probably a very controversial topic. And I must state before sharing my opinions that I am not judging anyone's choices, and I have great respect for single moms, for handling more than I think myself willing or capable of handling. The reason I'm bringing this up is that I have always believed that children come into their parents' life by choice, and that the way we raise our children is also by choice.

While I have a lot of respect for single mothers and I understand that some choose to be single, I was a little bit shocked when I first came to the U.S. and met a lot of single mothers who had more than 1 child – sometimes as many as 4, that all had different fathers. Growing up with a circle of friends who avoided having children too early in life, so as to take care of material things first, I was shocked to find such a disregard for prevention of pregnancy in a country that calls itself "the greatest country in the world".

Now, I'm not advocating abortion, though I do believe that is also a matter of personal choice and not national debate. I'm simply stating that there are a lot of ways to become pregnant for all those people engaged in short-term sexual relations. After more than a decade of life in a country where abortion was illegal and making babies highly encouraged – to the point that there were financial penalties for people who didn't have children – I believe very strongly in the power of personal choice in family matters. With that said, I also believe that all parents should have the child's best interest at heart when making decisions that will influence that child's life.

Lesson 5: WELFARE?

Once I met more than a few people whose livelihoods rely on welfare money coming in, I began to question the efficiency and the wisdom of the system. In my mind I associated the set up with the way "heroine mothers" (mothers of 3 or more children) were compensated by the communist regime. This remuneration encouraged a certain segment of the population to start bringing more babies into the world in order to increase revenue, with total disregard for the well-being of these children.

When I left Romania, and since I had already been out from under communist rule for many years, plus I was relocated to a country that had never had anything remotely close to a communist regime... I really didn't expect to run across these same stories on this side of the Atlantic.

On the other hand, when it comes to disability income and not money for having children, access to the funds is very difficult, and it can take a long time to even start receiving anything. Had an opportunity to hear horror stories about heart-breaking situations that people found themselves in, triggered by health problems. Bureaucracy at its magnificent best... or should I say worst?! And I thought I had left that behind. This was an unpleasant surprise.

Lesson 6: HEALTH CARE?

Since I have worked in the insurance field for many years, I got used to the terminology. I have come across two ways to express the term health insurance – medical insurance is sometimes used for the same product. I prefer the latter because I feel that the services that are covered pertain very little to maintaining one's health in good stead.

I grew up in a country where medical care was provided by the state during the communist regime, at no cost to the population. However, good medical care came only for the cost of whatever bribe required by the doctor treating you: it could be a pack of foreign cigarettes, some chocolate or even money. Post-communism, the practice of bribery continued, while the system was kept more or less in the same "no cost to the population" status. The main difference with time, was the beginning of a private – for-pay – system that developed; better care, more modern technology, and cleaner hospitals. All this came at a cost that not everyone could afford.

I remember numerous stories that were featured on TV about people, among them many children, who came on to appeal to anyone who could help them with money for life-saving procedures abroad. Many of them had the U.S. as the destination for their dream of a healthier life to come to fruition. The expectation on my part was that the medical system here was way more advanced and the doctors were both capable and willing to perform miracles in service to their patients.

Once I have lived here for a few years, I understood that the entire medical system is built on managing the level of disease and not designed to help people feel better longer, so they would not have to use the medical system. I have a client who frequently told me she didn't want to go see her doctor unless the situation was dire indeed; she felt that for every ache and pain he would prescribe a pill that she would then have to keep taking, even after the trouble was long gone. Granted, she is elderly. But I realized that I would not want to live my life tied to a handful of daily pills, even at her age. So, I can understand her reticence, and even agree and act the same way.

While growing up I only knew an elderly lady who had diabetes – type I, as I now can understand – and nobody among the adults surrounding me took any pills for high blood pressure. As part of my job with the life insurance company, I had to ask many a medical question, and probably roughly about half of the people I met had high blood pressure and were taking pills for it, and about a third had diabetes.

I'm not debating statistics, nor do I intend to get into a debate about the problem with health care, or lack thereof. My intent is to simply express my surprise and disappointment at the state of affairs in the U.S. when it comes to the health of its population.

Lesson 7: VOTING FOR THE PRESIDENT

Even though 2016 was a very hot year on the political front, with emotions running high on both sides, I'm not going to say anything pro or con the president – past, present or future. What I want to address is the voting system. The one thought and implemented by the Founding Fathers.

During the previous elections, I never heard as much talk about the way the Electoral College votes for the president, so I always thought the system too hard to figure out, and set up this way on purpose. But it didn't seem to influence the outcome of the elections too much, since it was pretty close to the popular vote from November. The last election spun that theory on its head though. So, I did some research and tried to understand it. But I must confess that I was unable to figure out how it really works. And now I'm wondering (again) if the system was built in such a complex and hard-to-understand way on purpose, so the average Joe and Jane have no idea how it works and therefore they cannot contest it.

I cannot help but remember the TV images from my youth when the president of Romania, a.k.a. the dictator, was voted unanimously by a group of party members representing the entire Communist Party in the national congress. Not that the Electoral College follows the same rules but to me is scary that a small group of people can determine who the president is. The Romanian people used to explain the election proceedings as "you vote whom you want, and the person who is supposed to win is the one elected" – meaning that the average voters have no say in who wins the elections.

In post-communist Romania, the president is elected in true democratic popular vote. To win, a candidate must have 50% of the votes plus one. Since there is usually a large number of candidates (many parties have a candidate of their own), there are many instances when no one can get the necessary votes. In this case, the top 2 candidates in the number of votes go to a second round – 2 weeks later or so – and the one with the most votes becomes the new president. The president may not be the best person to take the reins but it is the one the majority wants, in a truly democratic fashion.

***

As I put my words on paper, I am coming to understand that not all my readers will agree with the opinions I expressed in this book and especially in this last chapter. I know we all have the right to our own opinions and these are just mine. All I can do is thank you for taking the time to read them and share some moments of your life with me by allowing me to share my life story and the money lessons that I learned along the way.

I feel blessed and privileged to have had an opportunity to grow up in 2 different political systems, while surrounded by a loving family who always supported me while allowing me to make my decisions – as well as my mistakes. I crossed the Atlantic with an opinion about the world that was waiting for me at the other end of my flight; then I learned that the life seen through the windows can be very different from the life lived on the inside. I had to learn, and I had to adapt. And through it all, I grew into the person that I am today. I'm now different from the friends that I left back home because my background and experiences have molded me into a very different adult from the one that left Romania back in 2002. And I'm still very different from most of the new friends that I have made on this side of the Ocean, because they don't have the life experiences and the background that has brought me across the Atlantic.

While I'm still growing and learning, and there still are surprises all the time, I feel it is my duty to share some of my unique gifts and talents to help others, and also to share a perspective that may give some of my readers food for thought. So far, these are the 7 most puzzling lessons that have been revealed to me during my years here in the U.S.

Some things I'm still trying to get used to… some things I'm trying to navigate around… but with all of them, there is nothing else for me to do than to "suck it up, Buttercup!"

Acknowledgements:

This story came into print with the accountability of a great coach, Syndee Hendricks, and with encouragement from a wonderful friend, Diana Parra. I will always be grateful for your support and inspiration!

I would not have a lot to talk about if I had been born in a family that encouraged me to be the best I can be – I'm grateful to my parents and my aunt, who are always there for me, and to my grandparents who are my guardian angels. They always built my self-esteem up and supported my competitive spirit.

I will always be thankful for living in 2 different countries and building friendships on 2 continents because they keep me grounded and give me the motivation to achieve my dreams.

I learned the first business lessons by looking at successful people from afar – Zig Ziglar, Tony Robbins, Suze Orman and Robert Kiyosaki – and from up close – Rick Altig, Ilija Orlovic, Sandra Yancey and Steve Crawford.

My gratitude and my hope to serve others have given birth to this book. And I'm amazed on how the Universe is bringing the resources I need in my life to make sure the book becomes a reality. And I'm grateful for each and every single one of my readers.

Author's Bio

Sorana Blackfoot is a Prosperity Mentor, teaching women to create, preserve and transfer wealth. Through her company, Un-Broke Women, she advises women on building better relationships with their money.

Originally from Romania, Sorana has been living in Richmond, VA since 2002. Coming to a new country, she built a successful career to make it worth the sacrifice of uprooting herself.

During her 10+ years career in the financial industry, she learned that a lot of women are uncomfortable with their finances and therefore, are left in a very precarious situation if/when they are alone due to divorce or widowhood.

Sorana has coauthored 2 books in the last 2 years: "Remarkable Results" and "Goal for it!" and is now publishing her first individual book, an autobiography.

Sorana believes in empowering women to achieve financial serenity. Her mission is accomplished through books, classes, powerful Prosperity Circles, 1-on-1 consultations and a weekly podcast, "Money Mondays".

www.ingramcontent.com/pod-product-compliance
Lightning Source LLC
Chambersburg PA
CBHW071207220526
45468CB00002B/526